MW00416991

with
SIMPLE FAITH

RITA WOODARD

Dedicated to Karen Powell, who at the time of the writing of this book, is fighting ovarian cancer with steadfast faith in the power of asking God for healing.

In honor of my friend Matt Mosley with whom we share the bond of God's miraculous healing from cancer while we are still on this earth.

In memory of my friend Doug Dumpert who is with Jesus, where he has been completely healed for eternity.

Contents

.

Foreword

In James 4:2, the Bible says the reason we have not is that we ask not. Really? Is it really that easy? Yes, I believe it can be, and it only takes simple faith. When was the last time you asked God for something? I mean asked for just anything, believing with all your heart that He could provide—not necessarily that He *would,* but that He *could?* If your answer is that you are not really convinced, then your prayers may be empty. Faith is believing in a God you have not seen, and believing He actually can do anything. I have learned to ask God for things He can do through me, not just for me.

I believe, in the deepest part of my soul, God hears me when I make my requests known through prayer.

Your life can have more power once you accept Jesus Christ as your Saviour. God has worked powerfully in my life, and He can do the same for you. Through simple faith, He healed me when I was at death's door, and provided for me when I was in need.

If we expect God to work in our lives, there are some things we can do to increase our faith and realize His awesome power. My confidence in God hearing and answering prayer grows when I:

- humble myself
- believe that God can do anything
- ask Him for what I need through sincere prayer
- am willing to accept His answer
- thank Him for His answer

I know these five steps seem simple; however, when implemented into your daily life, you will be amazed at how God will work. They have brought me to an intimate place with Him. He has taken away my Martha-like anxiety about many things and replaced it with His peace and confidence (Luke 10:41, 42).

In today's world, Satan uses a lack of humility and obedience to keep us from asking God for what we need. Our high-tech world keeps us too busy to hear His answers. Many have become self-reliant, and blind to the true power of God's ability and desire to provide for us. Humility, faith and obedience have opened the door to ask God for everything I need. I have seen God move mountains in my life. You can too!

My hope is to encourage you in the deepest part of your soul to believe that with God, **all** things are possible. In Luke 18:27, Jesus tells us that the things which are impossible with men are possible with God. Please join me as we travel down a road that reveals the **provision** and **power** of God that comes with **ASKING GOD in simple faith.**

Acknowledgments

To My Father God

My Heavenly Father who taught me to ask Him for everything I need and has put HIS desires in MY heart

To My Mother and Father

Mama: the diligent woman who read her Bible every day and set an example for me to know the power of prayer to God, our Father, through Jesus Christ

Daddy: the man who worked hard and provided for me as a child; the one who taught me to appreciate every little thing God gives us

To My Husband

Herbert: the man I love and the man who loves me unconditionally; the one who knows that I hear the voice of God and always encourages me to obey it

To My Daughters and Their Families

Kelly and Andy; Drew, Adam, Kyle
Abby and Nathan; Dylan and Easton
who I pray will always know the great love and blessings of our Heavenly Father throughout their lives

Chapter 1

My Leap of Faith

*II Corinthians 5:7—For we walk
by faith, not by sight.*

Decisions! Decisions! Decisions! I felt that all I did
every day in my job was make one decision after
another. My life was jam-packed with tension, stress
and decisions. When I took a rare moment to look
around me, I wasn't alone. There were others–so
many others in the same boat.

What happened to the days when I would sit on
our back deck after dinner, and watch the kids play
outside? I would sip sweet tea and perhaps enjoy a
visit from my neighbor. Were those simple, pleasant
days gone forever? Ambition and technology had tied

me to a cell phone and proverbial umbilical cord of an always present laptop. The emails were endless and relaxation was hard to find.

During family vacations, I often told my family I needed more time before I'd join them on the beach. As soon as the door closed behind them, I'd get my laptop and cell phone and get to work. The moment I plugged in to my laptop, I was emotionally back in the office; I felt such a devotion to my career. It was taking up so much of my time and energy that it was distracting me from the relationship with my family which should have been the priority.

For many years I enjoyed my job in the corporate world. Yet, it was demanding and I began to feel as if I wasn't ever fully "in the moment" anywhere at any given time, because my to-do list at work was endless. I never wanted to leave anything unfinished at work.

In my personal life, I wanted to be a faithful Christian, good wife, mother and grandmother. I wanted to do everything the very best I could in both worlds. Life was like a juggling act with too many work-related balls in the air. Something desperately needed to change. Now.

I started asking God to help me to achieve balance in my life again. I was staying up until 3:00 a.m. most nights overwhelmed with work. I began to feel so discouraged, because my job was dominating my time and virtually ruling my life. I finally cried out to God in a heart-rending, fervent prayer asking Him to deliver me from the controlling reign my career had over my life. God heard me. He answered me. What happened next was nothing short of a miracle! When I gave up my out-of-balance life to God in prayer, things rapidly began to change.

It all began in 2010, when my company with 90,000 employees, created a **new one-of-a-kind position**. Our vice-president called me and asked me to apply for this wonderful position within our company. I was so honored. I sensed God may have orchestrated this amazing opportunity just for me. I was humbled to think of how my Father in Heaven cared about every detail of my life.

My husband, Herbert, was very supportive and excited about the new potential position. He prayed with me as we sought God's will, and he encouraged me to follow God's leading. He is such a supportive husband, and the best friend I could ask for in life.

Ten long months after I applied, a final decision was made for this brand new position. Thankfully, it was awarded to me. The Lord had answered my prayers. With hope and excitement in my heart, I met my new team, Monte, Deb, and Regina. We immediately formed a very strong bond. We felt confident we had the right combination for a great team. We had such respect for one another as Christians, and developed a very deep friendship.

Later, with some restructuring, Monte was moved to a different position, and Fletcher replaced him. In 2013, Lance joined us, and the five of us became an unstoppable, winning team. What happened next was unprecedented in our company.

Together, we signed over **forty million dollars in new business contracts in a matter of months**. It just seemed everything we touched turned to gold. After so many years of working diligently, I was at the height of my career in a dream job that God had created just for me. I was busy, but I was also content.

Herbert was living the dream on our farm, training quarter horses, and working with local farmers as a hay broker. He had been self-employed for about ten years.

Now, it seemed life was absolutely perfect; however, God actually had a totally different plan for me.

God began to unfold this new plan for my life through a Bible study group. My dear friend, Gail Wrather, invited me to join her in a ladies Bible study led by our friend, Judy Reed. Her timing was perfect, because I felt like I needed to be involved in an organized study of God's Word. Also, I needed to reconnect with good Christian friends.

I decided to make a commitment to the study. This was one of the best decisions I had ever made. It was such a blessing to be part of such a faithful group of women. I could actually feel myself growing spiritually every day. It was such a special intimate time as we gathered each week to laugh and cry together, as we shared what God was revealing to us.

We first studied *Ruth: Loss, Love and Legacy* (written by Kelly Minter). We studied the direction Ruth took in her life and how God blessed her; yet, it was not what would have made sense to most of us.

Ruth 1:8–19 tells us that after Ruth's husband died, she didn't return to her mother's house and the security of her own people. She stayed to take care of her distressed mother-in-law, Naomi. How many of us would do that? Ruth was faithful to her mother-in-law who was going to be alone without her. In Ruth 1:16, she tells Naomi, "thy people shall be my people, and thy God my God." She followed the direction the Lord gave her, and He richly blessed her. She met Boaz, their love blossomed, and they got married.

Following God's leadership is not always easy, but it is always right. Ruth was a wonderful example for all of us.

Each day as I studied, and every Wednesday morning when our Bible study group met, the Holy Spirit began to use Ruth's example to speak to me. I began to consider making a change in my life. A big change. I began to think about leaving my wonderful secure job. I would see glimpses of a new path in my life that would require me to walk by faith and not by sight.

Would God really orchestrate the perfect job for me, and then want me to leave it?

There was a tugging on my heartstrings that my life needed to change. Thoughts would come to mind that challenged where I was spending my time. I began to feel a very strong calling by The Lord to invest my time in things eternal, rather than the materialistic things here on earth. I needed more quiet time with Jesus one on one. I yearned to know Him better. I felt the need to put my spiritual gifts to use with hospitality, sharing my home, cooking and caring more for the needs of others. It was difficult to consider this idea as much of our livelihood hinged on my salary and all of the benefits my job secured.

Still, when we completed the workbook and Bible study I continued to feel very unsettled. Through our study, the Holy Spirit of God seemed to show me I was missing a calling in my life.

My desires strangely began to change. The great importance I had placed on success at my fabulous job began to wane. God was showing me that I should slow the pace of my life so I could see the real needs of others. Was I really seeing the needs of my husband, my children, my grandchildren? What was I missing and why?

I began to question my motives for being so dependent on my job. It was time to quit running wide open, and just start listening closer to God. Really listening. I realized that being "busy" was just a tool of Satan that was being used to keep me from having deeper relationships with God, and with my family and friends.

The Lord was leading me by the hand as His child. I knew I could trust Him. Romans 8:14 says, "For as many as are led by the Spirit of God, they are the sons of God." I prayerfully asked Him to align my heart with His plan.

Our next Bible study workbook was *Nehemiah: A Heart That Can Break* (written by Kelly Minter). What a fascinating study of one man's prayers and sacrifice! Nehemiah held a good position as the king's cupbearer in the comfort of his Persian palace. God called him away to do **His** work. Yes. **He left his job to do what God was calling him to do.** This hit very close to home for me.

It all began with Nehemiah's surrendered heart. He was burdened by the poor and oppressed who were in need. He was called to rebuild the wall around Jerusalem for their security and strength. Wow! I was in awe of Nehemiah's obedience and focus. He was determined to obey God, and nothing could distract him. I was inspired when I read in Nehemiah 6:15 that the wall was finished in fifty-two days. I once heard God doesn't use great people to do great things, he uses **surrendered people**.

Through this study, I came to know that God blesses our surrender. Nehemiah's surrendered heart taught us that our breaking hearts are often what God uses to restore broken people.

I knew the Lord was speaking directly to me to follow Nehemiah's example and make some huge changes. Soon. As I pondered my life, I came to know with more conviction that my calling was to surrender the secure shelter of my career.

We need to know we can **ask God** for what we need and **we can trust Him to answer us**. He has proven this to me over and over.

So why was this so hard for me?

I am a simple woman with a simple faith. I believe God can do anything. He can do great things **through us** when we demonstrate our faith in Him through our obedience to Him. Faith doesn't come with a blueprint of His plans. I had simply to trust Him.

Leaving my job was going to require great obedience.

As I began to ponder the idea of going from a six-figure income to an income of **zero**, I got a lump in my throat. I also pondered losing **all** of our insurance coverage for medical, dental, vision, life insurance, 401K, etc. Now exactly why would I want to give up all of this? No part of this concept seemed logical or reasonable.

In the past, there was nothing logical about the decisions I made when following God's lead. This time was no different. As I sat on my back deck late one evening, I tried to understand the reason God would want me to do something so financially irresponsible. I poured out my questions and doubts in prayer. Then a still, small voice spoke to me in the most sacred depths of my heart, and said I needed to write my life story. It seemed like it would be impossible for me to pick up a pen and try to corral my thoughts into a logical sequence in a book. I wondered why He would want me to do this?

I know God had compassion for my confusion. The Holy Spirit impressed deep within me that if I didn't write it then, when I die, all the miracles He'd done for me would be buried with me. If I do tell about His faithfulness to me, He will receive the glory for all He has done. Someone could be encouraged by God's healing and provision in my life. It all suddenly made sense. Out of my weakness would come His strength and victory.

At first I was overwhelmed because I didn't know where to begin. God led our Bible study group into a new study, *Gideon: Your Weakness, God's Strength* (written by Priscilla Shirer). Gideon was called to a task that seemed impossible. I empathized with Gideon, because it seemed crazy that I would quit my job. God slowly revealed to me His plan, and made it clear. He would carry me through. He reassured me, just as He did Gideon in Judges 6:16, that He would be with me. The task would require my complete trust in God through my personal, intimate relationship with Him.

Like Gideon, I felt ill-equipped for such a big task. Yet we find in Judges 7:16, Gideon's small army used trumpets, empty pitchers, and torches to defeat the Midianites' large army. The one thing that Gideon and I both had was the power of the Lord. Romans 8:31 confirmed to me that if God is for us, who can be against us? My weakness would give God the opportunity to show His strength. God equipped me with His Holy Spirit, with the Bible, with prayer, truth, faith and humility.

"We can do this," God said to me, and through the quietness of the moment, **I knew that I had to trust and obey. I knew if I walked in faith like Gideon had, then God would provide.**

The Lord began convincing me that I needed to align my heart with His plan for my life. He impressed on me not to think of what I would be missing, but what I could give and do for others. I set my eyes on the promises He had made to me. I had to prepare to let go. God would re-prioritize my life and provide a new set of parameters within which I would live.

God's timing seemed to be calling me with urgency. There couldn't be a "wait until you're sixty-two and can draw social security." No, instead I just opened my Bible and my eyes went directly to II Corinthians 5:7, where I was instructed to "walk by faith, not by sight." I knew His Word would be the lamp to my feet and the light to my path going into my future. I would have to depend on His care and provisions, rather than my own career path.

As we had studied Ruth, Nehemiah, and Gideon, I began to focus on the fact they all had walked by faith and not by sight. Faith. Simple faith.

As I sat in my chair reading my Bible on the morning of February 3, 2014, I asked God to speak to me clearly as to why I would have to give up my job when it didn't seem like a very responsible move on my part. He whispered to my heart, "I gave you this job, and it has been exactly what you have needed. Now I have a new path for you to follow, but to open the gate to this new direction, you will have to lay your job on the altar of sacrifice and surrender." God said, **"I will not take it from you. You have to give it to Me willingly."**

This troubled me because none of this was the way I had planned it. Still, I had proof He would provide. I had been asking God for everything I needed since I was twenty-five years old. Now He was asking me for one thing; to lay down my job and my security, and to walk completely by faith for His provision and providence.

I cried as I fell to my knees and said, "Yes, Lord, I lay at Jesus's feet my job that provides our financial security and so many other benefits. You have been so faithful to me, and I will be obedient to You." This was one of the hardest decisions I had ever made, but I knew the Lord had spoken.

When Herbert awoke, I told him what I'd experienced. Without reservation he said, "You've got to trust God. If that's what He said to do, that is what we need to do."

It's a blessing to have the full support of a Christian husband who shares the same heart for God's will in our lives. We had to prepare for me to leave my company. Even though we would be more comfortable with me working a few more years, a few months would just have to do for us.

As I did my job each day, I continued to have overwhelming, almost supernatural success. We were completing the rollout of the six-million-dollar contract we'd won that fall when our "Dream Team" landed a brand new fifteen-million-dollar contract. It was the largest contract in this product category in the history of our company's healthcare division. Excitement and celebration of this huge win became the chatter of our company. Even so, the time came, and though it was difficult, I gave notice I'd be leaving the company. It seemed like a totally insane decision in light of the recent overwhelming successes.

I just knew I had to be obedient. God spoke to me about a new way of living my life. Thoughts of leaving the green pastures that had provided everything we needed for the last thirty years were daunting. I was about to walk through a gate into a place that, by human reasoning offered no income and no insurance. It meant relying fully on my husband's horse and hay business.

The "what-ifs" began to flood my mind. You can only imagine how fear tried to overtake me as I thought of our unstable economy and the unforeseen things life brings. Yet Jesus, my Shepherd, picked me up in His loving arms and wrapped them around this little, scared lamb. He whispered softly to my heart, "You will have more time to spend with Me. Obey Me. Do exactly what I have told you to do when I have told you to do it. Be obedient to My voice. I will carry you. I will never leave you nor will I ever forsake you. I am the Good Shepherd."

I felt my Shepherd's arms tightly hold me, as I walked through the next months. I knew it was the Holy Spirit of God leading me to a new place. It was a time of sacrifice that required I walk by faith, and not by sight. A place with no pride or ambition. I simply wanted God's perfect peace that comes from obedience. I had recently heard a quote that rang in my ears, "In life, our greatest fear shouldn't be of failure, but of succeeding at things that don't really matter." I knew I wanted to succeed in things with eternal value, not in things in the corporate world.

With only weeks to go before my final day of employment, the country's largest healthcare system signed a twenty-million-dollar contract with me that we had been working on over the past few months. As a result, I continued to get phone calls from our company's top executives, who asked me to stay. The offers were flanked by large, attractive pay raises and more benefits. I listened to their words and carefully considered what they had to say. On a Monday morning, I had a call with another attractive escalated offer. I asked myself, "Wow, are they really talking to me?" The offer seemed too good to be true.

As soon as I hung up the phone agreeing to ponder the offer, my phone again rang. It was my friend Charlene Taylor. She said she felt a sudden urgency to call me and encouraged me to listen to the voice of God. She prayed to God on my behalf, **boldly asking Him to provide strength and courage for me to follow His leading in my life.**

It was God's perfect timing. Charlene encouraged me to fix my eyes not on what I can see, but on what is unseen. She said I should not wonder what is on the road ahead, I should concentrate and entrust myself to God's watch care. After Charlene's reinforcing phone call, God, once again, wrapped His arms around me and assured me I needed more time with Him, not money or a prestigious position. He reminded me that He would be our Provider, as we aligned our lives with His will. God is Jehovah-Jireh, the Lord who provides (Genesis 22:8, 12–14). I truly felt my calling was to pursue the things the Lord had for me to do.

With continuing prayer for all I needed in order to meet each enticing phone call from my company, I would respond with appreciation, but refuse the offer. Total peace would engulf me, as I declined the generous offers.

Then, suddenly, as my final day of employment approached, Satan launched an all-out attack on my life. That morning, darts of doubt came from all directions. Fear engulfed me as I thought, "What in the world am I doing? What will we do for insurance?" "What-ifs" raged through me, and I trembled in fear.

I was miserable, but God saw me in my pitiful state of mind, and appointed my friend Susanne Adams to cross my path that afternoon. I told her how I was feeling. She said, "Rita, I have never seen you like this. You are under Satan's attack." I knew she was right. Then she gently took my hand and prayed mightily with authority for me as she asked God to defeat Satan, and drive him far from me. She asked God to restore my faith and confidence to follow what He has directed me to do. Through trembling and tears, I reclaimed the power of God in my life. Just as quickly as the fear had come, it left. Peace, once again, reigned in my heart, and Satan had lost the battle.

God defeated Satan through the powerful prayers of my dear friend. He removed the pride and ambition that Satan tried to slip back into my heart.

The effectual fervent prayer of a righteous man availeth much.—James 5:16

It is so important for us to be sensitive to others and recognize their needs and then lift those needs up to our Father. I was thankful that Susanne and I were able to see each other that day. She has been a godly example for me and many other women to follow. She has given God the glory for every blessing in her life.

The Lord certainly works in mysterious ways. I had never been a morning person; however, God began to wake me at 5:30 each morning to start writing this book. I never once had to use an alarm clock. He would nudge me, and I would slip out of bed to go directly to get my cup of hot coffee, my Bible, my pen, and pad. He gave me a Scripture: "My voice shalt thou hear in the morning, O Lord; in the morning will I direct my prayer unto thee, and will look up" (Psalm 5:3). Each day as I prayed, studied His Word and listened to Him, the words would come to my heart so that I could pen them. I know that He enabled me because I was incapable of doing this without Him.

When my final day of employment came and the retirement parties were over, I said my goodbyes. It was bittersweet to end my thirty-year career that had provided so much for us. For many years, it had helped define who I was when my heart was full of ambition. Now I was walking away, leaving it behind and asking God **to define who I was in Him.**

God replaced my worldly ambition with thoughts of eternal treasures. I look forward to the day when I can lay my treasures at Jesus' feet. He gave me a sense of satisfaction, confidence and reaffirmation far above and beyond that which could be derived from or controlled by any paycheck or secure benefits.

Chapter 2

Simple Beginnings

Proverbs 22:6—Train up a child in the way he should go: and when he is old, he will not depart from it.

My parents were compassionate, caring, salt-of-the-earth Christians. They had four children when they bought a lovely forty-acre farm in Murfreesboro, Tennessee. There, they built a white-shingled home suitable for a family of six. Shortly after they settled in, Linda and I were born. By today's standards, the home was a bit small for the eight of us, yet we all loved it dearly.

As long as I stayed out of trouble, being the youngest meant I had it pretty easy. My imaginary friend, Hockeybean, and I would go play in my tiny utopian world. I loved everything about growing up on a farm, especially the fragrance of the hyacinths in the spring and capturing fireflies in Mason jars in the summertime. I would wake early to the smell of the southern honeysuckle that climbed wildly over our fences. The fragrance was wonderful, but I loved the taste best. I would pick a handful of blooms, then delicately bite the stem and suck out the delicious honey.

It was our family tradition in early July to go blackberry picking. It was a highlight of our summer. My brothers, sisters and I were equipped with gallon buckets, and we would pick and pick until the sun's heat forced us to go back to the house. After lunch, we girls would head to the shade trees in the yard to cap the berries to get them ready for Mama to make cobblers, jams, and preserves. Mama was always cooking, and our home was always warm and welcoming. In the evenings, we played rummy, rook, and checkers.

There were joys inside and out, and my child's heart was always full of love and happiness. We made a lot of sweet memories. Mama and Daddy saw to it we faithfully attended church three times a week. Daddy served as a deacon. Mama cooked a special Sunday lunch every week. Occasionally, we invited the preacher and his family over after church to join us. Sunday was my favorite day of the week!

As a child, I fondly remember a secure feeling in my heart that all was well with the world. Our life was like an episode of *The Waltons*. Life on the farm was good. It seemed we had it all. My parents lived by the philosophy found in Proverbs 22:6: "Train up a child in the way he should go: and when he is old, he will not depart from it." Rearing Christian children was their number one priority. They gave us a solid foundation on which to build our lives.

My mother was a homemaker, who cooked three meals a day, kept a spotless home with shiny hardwood floors, and read her Bible every day of the week. She was a diligent, loving mother. People were drawn to her because of her accepting nature. She was fun to be around and had a dry sense of humor. Wherever she went and whomever she met, people just seemed to love her.

My father was stern, but his heart was as soft as new fallen snow. He worked hard and was a good provider. He loved to garden, golf, and fish. He was good at all of them. He treasured the little things in life and made life a lot of fun for us.

My oldest sister, Janice, always took an interest in playing with me, pretending I was her baby. I adored her. Being with her was my secure, happy place. Actually being with all my brothers and sisters was my favorite thing in the whole world.

I also enjoyed visiting our neighbors, the Smythe family. I vividly recall walking across the field between our farms on warm summer mornings. The sparkling dew lay on the soft blue morning glories that God displayed beautifully along the fence that I would cross to get to their house.

Susan Smythe was a close friend, but it was actually her mother who truly made an impact on my life. Mrs. Smythe welcomed me into her home, where the windows were usually open to circulate fresh breezes. First Peter 4:9 says we are to show hospitality to each other. She definitely had the gift of hospitality. She was a teacher and always wanted to teach me something. She encouraged me by telling me I was smart and fun to teach.

By the time I was five years old, she had taught me all of my addition, subtraction, and most of my multiplication facts. She helped me memorize so many things, just by spending time with me and caring so deeply about me. Years later, when I attended Central High School, she was my Latin teacher. I can still see her face in my mind's eye and hear her scratchy voice. Many people thought she was a bit eccentric, but I loved her and will always cherish her memory. She was a pivotal person in my childhood.

People never know how they are affecting the lives of children. I told myself as a child that I wanted to listen to little children when I grew up and to never forget how it felt to be heard. The Bible tells us that Jesus loves children. Matthew 19:14 tells us how He wanted them to come to Him. He always treated the children with love and kindness. It is so important to listen to what they have to say and to let them know we value them. Jesus is approachable and always has time for us. As adults, He wants us to come to Him as the little children did and spend quality time with Him.

When I was twelve years old, I wanted to be baptized. I had reached the age of accountability and knew the difference between right and wrong. My heart raced at the thought of going to Hell, so I nervously walked down the aisle of my church on a Sunday morning in fear. I thought it was what my church had taught me to do. I was thankful for my decision to be baptized because somehow I felt better, but something was still missing. I didn't develop a personal relationship with Jesus at this point. I was just doing what I thought I should do. I tried to be a good Christian by being good, in hopes of going to Heaven if I died. I had not been taught that salvation is a gift from God through Jesus. I was taught a works-based faith and wasn't at all secure in my salvation. How could I ever be good enough?

After my baptism, many things in my life began to change. I began to try too hard. I didn't really ever feel good enough. I don't know exactly how to describe it, but something was missing. Then, out of the blue, our family's life took a sharp turn. As I headed into my teen years, everything secure and wonderful in my life suddenly changed.

We sold our home on the beautiful farm on which I had lived since birth. Daddy thought it was time to downsize. He took early retirement, and we relocated to a cute brick home on three acres. He was only in his early fifties, but as his health began to fail, he seemed so old to me. This was the beginning of his congestive heart failure, which eventually resulted in two heart attacks.

After the first heart attack, Daddy experienced some depression. His failing health brought a new dynamic into our home. He was so different. He was impatient and he seemed worried about everything. He even cried at times. I loved my daddy and didn't want to be a burden to him. I felt guilty asking him for anything, anything at all. Nagging feelings of guilt welled up inside me. I began to think I should provide essential things myself. So at fourteen, I went to work at an ice cream shop on Friday nights and Sunday afternoons. I then got a second job working concessions at a movie theater on weeknights. I adjusted the best I could and made lots of new friends at my new school. However, sadly, I didn't make any close friends at our new church.

I grew up fast. I felt different from my friends whose parents were there to supply all of their needs. I didn't feel I could ask my parents for anything. I developed a very independent spirit. I was determined to succeed and do my best at everything! I thought if I didn't expect anything from anyone then I could be happy with everyone, everywhere, all of the time. My personal goals couldn't be achieved by depending on others. I had my own agenda and work to do. I wanted to get it right, do my very best, and not be concerned with what I didn't have. I felt like a one-girl team and became extremely independent.

Deep inside I began to feel like I was alone on an island and learned to depend solely on myself. I bought an old car and got my own insurance. I bought my clothes, gas and the things a sixteen-year-old girl thinks she needs. I was crazy busy. Most of the time, I was too busy to stop and listen to the Lord, but thankfully my mother's prayers were always going before me.

Sometimes my goal of excellence for myself was too high. I was driven from a place deep inside to excel. That sounds like a good thing, but I couldn't find contentment because I always thought I could have done better.

Life began to move into the fast lane for me. My mother never learned to drive, so transportation was hard to come by until I was sixteen. We did not live in the city, but all of my new friends did, so I stayed with my friends more than I stayed at home. I was on the go most of the time with school, church, work, and friends. I was blessed to have wonderful friends.

My blessings were multiplied because my dear friends had such loving parents, who always welcomed me into their homes. My friends, Debbie and Judy, had that kind of parents. I stayed at their house so much, they actually made me my own little closet in their den. They shared their home and meals with me, but most of all, their sweet mother, Ann, shared her love and hospitality like no other. Also, Aunt Hallie, my cousin Susan's mother, always welcomed me into her home too. She was a wonderful southern cook, and she always made me feel welcome at her table.

School was my greatest joy. I loved it! A deep need to do my best at school drove me. I usually made all A's, and then signed my own report cards. Mama never even looked at them, because she had her hands full taking care of things at home with Daddy.

I wasn't given rules, so I made my own. I watched my friends' parents. I noticed they would ground their children for doing things they shouldn't. I wanted to be grounded so badly, I decided to ground myself one weekend. I figured I deserved it for doing something I shouldn't have done.

When my mother came into my room that Friday, she asked if I was sick. I told her I just didn't feel well. It actually felt great to be grounded, but I couldn't bring myself to tell her. When my friends called me throughout the weekend, I told them I couldn't go anywhere because I was grounded. I felt cool to have a boundary like my friends, even if it was self-imposed. Throughout my young life, I created my own boundaries, which was pretty scary.

My parents were older than my friends' parents. They seemed out of touch to me, but my mother knew a lot more than I thought she did at the time.

In my junior year of school, I went to work in a local flower shop thirty hours a week in order to have more income. I had a lot of responsibilities and it was a tough schedule to keep. I had to juggle a heavy workload along with schoolwork. Somewhat prematurely, I was on my own in making decisions. My mother tried to keep up with where I was but couldn't, so she eventually quit trying. I knew she was always behind the scenes, praying for my sister Linda and myself. All of the other siblings were grown by the time she and I were in high school.

I loved my classmates and my teachers, so I involved myself in as many things with them as possible. School was such a blessing to me.

Do you remember how everything was such a big deal when you were a teenager? I certainly remember how I felt during those exciting years. I recall a time when I came home all excited that I had been voted sophomore homecoming attendant. My mother began to fret, as she asked me where I would get a dress, shoes, and other things I would need for the event. I had no idea and neither did she.

I am confident she began to pray right then. There is nothing more powerful than a praying mother. She worried a lot, but she prayed more. She had been such a great mother with lots of rules for all of my older siblings, but now everything in our world had changed. She had to trust God to take care of me.

It seemed that out of the clear blue sky, someone I barely knew offered help. It was the freshman attendant, Kathy. She said her mother wanted me to ride with them to Nashville to get me a dress when she went to get hers. How could she have known how great my need was, and would she ever know what a blessing she was to me? I was thrilled. Mama knew it was an answer to her prayers. Peggy, Kathy's mother, helped me pick out a beautiful, sky-blue satin southern belle dress. It was perfect for the occasion. I felt like a princess.

Then there was the matter of how to get to the homecoming game. My boyfriend was supposed to pick me up that night and take me. Unfortunately, at the last minute, his mom called and said he wasn't feeling well and wouldn't be able to pick me up. Panic set in immediately. Thankfully my brother, Eddie, and his girlfriend, Jullie, rescued me. They picked me up in Eddie's Plymouth Barracuda fastback. It didn't have a backseat. Imagine me in my satin dress and spiral curls with no place to sit but the back floorboard of his car. My mother, the creative one, placed a lawn chair in the space where the backseat should have been. Even with my hoop skirt, somehow I awkwardly managed.

When we arrived, I leapt from the back of the two-door car. Eddie and Jullie drove away. Sadly, not one family member was there to share my excitement, but I just couldn't worry about all of that. I was so very thankful that my brother had been kind enough to bring me and get me there on time. The other girls on the court arrived in nice cars, with their parents, all with cameras and video equipment in hand. There was so much excitement, and the parents were all taking pictures of their daughters. I was alone—no pictures, no videos, just me—but might I add, a thankful, grateful me!

God saw my needs and supplied them! Nobody around me that special night knew I didn't have as much as any of the other girls on that court.

I was so proud just to be there, and my heart was full of happiness. My classmates had liked me enough to vote for me to represent our class. What more could I want? My friends gave me a ride home that night and I didn't have a single picture made by my family, but I have one in my heart of my friends' love and the Lord's provisions.

Life is not about what we don't have; it is about appreciating what we do have. Somehow I always knew that love was the most important thing in life. God was always out ahead of me making the way for me.

Chapter 3

My Heavenly Father

*Romans 5:8—But God
commendeth his love toward us,
in that, while we were yet
sinners, Christ died for us.*

As the years ticked by, I was striving and struggling
to do everything right. I began to feel as though I was
failing miserably. The more I tried to do things
perfectly, the more insecure I became. I felt quite
inadequate in many areas of my life. I was doing
things that I knew were not pleasing to God. I held
myself to a very high standard when I was young; but
then I began to make a lot of compromising
decisions.

My life seemed so difficult. Even though I thought I had become a Christian, it seemed hard because I had been taught that the only way to go to Heaven was to live my life every day doing everything right. How would I ever be able to do that? When I did things wrong and sinned (which I did frequently), I would ask for forgiveness. God would forgive me; yet I would turn around and do those same things again. I felt very much like the apostle Paul when he wrote Romans 7:15–25. He would do the very things he hated, and his flesh struggled against his spirit.

My core problem was that I had a works-based faith, so I didn't have any assurance of my salvation. I felt guilty about everything I did and never felt "good enough." There was no peace in my heart. Everything looked fine on the outside, but I was in a state of turmoil on the inside. I married a man named Eddie at age twenty and had a precious baby girl, Kelly, at age twenty-two. It all seemed like a perfectly happy life, but something was missing. Where was the peace and confidence of God? I didn't have them, and I didn't know why. I was going through life acting like one person on the outside while it seemed there was a different person on the inside. There was an acute sense of dissonance in my spirit.

My heart cringed at the voices I would hear within me. They seemed to say, "You are not good enough and never will be. You will go to Hell when you die.

You are not doing enough. You have unforgiven sin in your life." This unrest ruled inside me. You never know what is really in someone's heart. I seemed to be fine by the world's standards because I hid my inner struggles.

My insecurities continued; then (**praise the Lord)** in church on a Sunday night about three years later, God mercifully gave me assurance of my salvation through a sermon based on Scriptures from the Book of Titus.

> *"Not by works of righteousness which we have done, but according to his mercy he saved us, by the washing of regeneration, and renewing of the Holy Ghost; Which he shed on us abundantly through Jesus Christ our Saviour."*—Titus 3:5, 6.

I listened and finally understood for the first time what it meant to be saved and have a **personal relationship** with Jesus, my Saviour.

I realized God loved me. "For God so loved the world, that he gave his only begotten Son, that whosoever believeth in him should not perish, but have everlasting life" (John 3:16). Yes, He loved me in a personal way. I knew it deep in my soul.

I realized I was a sinner with a boatload of sin. "For all have sinned, and come short of the glory of

God" (Romans 3:23). I could finally see how ugly my sin was and knew I needed a Saviour.

I realized that my sin had a price that had to be paid. "For the wages of sin is death; but the gift of God is eternal life through Jesus Christ our Lord" (Romans 6:23). My good works are not a part of salvation. Salvation is a gift from God.

I prayed and asked Jesus to be my Saviour and I knew for sure, for the first time ever, that I would go to Heaven when I die. "That if thou shalt confess with thy mouth the Lord Jesus, and shalt believe in thine heart that God hath raised him from the dead, thou shalt be saved" (Romans 10:9).

Things changed for me on that wonderful night when I realized it was God's mercy and grace that saved me, not my good or bad deeds. I was sitting on the back pew of a Baptist church when God spoke to my heart and I heard Him whisper to me, "You are **My** child, and I am **your** Father. You can trust Me and ask Me for anything you need." **A sudden joy and peace filled my heart because God's desire for my life was not for me to be independent but to be fully dependent upon Him and to trust Jesus for my salvation.** All God wanted was complete openness and transparency before Him.

I realized that God gave the gift of salvation through my faith and acceptance of Jesus' death, burial and resurrection. Salvation for my soul was not based on what I did or didn't do. It was based on what Jesus Christ did when He willingly gave His life on a cruel cross for me. Once I accepted His gift of salvation, I gained confidence that Heaven would be my home when I died.

I received blessed assurance that faith in Jesus made me a joint heir with Him. Knowing God was my Heavenly Father helped me to understand Him. He owns the cattle on a thousand hills (Psalm 50:10); and as my Father, He can certainly provide everything I might ever need.

Once again I felt what I had felt as a little girl; I had a Father who loved me and wanted me to depend wholly on His provisions. All along God had meant for the provision of my earthly father when I was a child to be a picture of my Heavenly Father now. All I had to do was have faith and ask Him.

I knew that I was forever changed from that moment. I had found the road to God's grace.

After that night, I placed my future in His hands without any fear. The unrest and insecurity were replaced by a deep peace inside me. I started asking God to help me with everything, and He did! Whatever I needed to know, He would tell me. Whatever I needed, He would provide for me.

Ephesians 1:18 says, *"The eyes of your understanding being enlightened; that ye may*

*know what is the hope of his calling, and what
the riches of the glory of his inheritance in the
saints."*

My trust in Him became real to me as I claimed my
position as God's child. My heart acknowledged the
inheritance that came with it according to Ephesians
1:10b-12. It was a vast, boundless inheritance that I
did not earn or deserve. I could experience true joy
and a consuming power within me.

I knew I could trust the character and love of God
with my simple faith.

Chapter 4

The Beginning of Obedience

Jeremiah 31:18—Thou hast chastised me, and I was chastised, as a bullock unaccustomed to the yoke: turn thou me, and I shall be turned; for thou art the LORD my God.

God had been so faithful to meet our family's needs. At age twenty-five, I realized He had done so much for me, and I began to ask myself the question, "What am I doing for Him?" I began to use part of my quiet time to find out what He wanted from me. It was time to start listening closer to hear His voice. I knew it was time to start giving back to God. He had my heart, but what about my obedience?

I had begun drinking socially as a teenager, but I was now beginning to hear the voice of God whispering that I should give it up totally, and start teaching a Sunday school class. I knew my social drinking was not bringing Him glory, but was it really such a big deal? I thought back to the teachings of my mother, who always said nothing good ever comes from drinking any kind of alcoholic beverage. Mama and Daddy set a good example for us to follow as parents, and I wanted to give my daughter the same heritage. God continued to impress on me that my social drinking was not pleasing to Him. Also, God continued to impress on me drinking was keeping me from the peace and power that come from complete obedience to Him.

Satan wanted me to ignore God's voice and my mother's example. He tempted me by saying that I worked hard, and deserved a few drinks to help me unwind. A little social drinking seemed harmless and he knew I really enjoyed it, but deep in my heart, I knew I wanted to be different. God wanted me to be "different" from the world. This is where I could begin to live the abundant Christian life to its full capacity.

I thought back to when I was a child. I was strongly influenced by ladies like Mrs. Thompson, my Sunday school teacher. She never took a drink in her life. I admired her, and I remember thinking that someday I wanted to grow up and be a Sunday school teacher like her. I wanted to smile at children with kind eyes and tell them about Jesus and His love for them.

Mrs. Thompson was also my mother's personal friend. She was truly a Proverbs 31 lady! When I was a little girl, we would go to visit her in her picturesque home that was nestled on a hillside with lots of shade trees along the Stones River. She was so thoughtful, and seemed always to have a piece of Juicy Fruit gum to give me. I know she couldn't have baked an apple pie every time we visited, but it seemed like she did. Her house always smelled so yummy. Her complexion was fair with chubby, rosy cheeks.

She and my mother would sit in her kitchen and talk about grownup stuff, but she would show that she cared about me too. She would bring me a *McCall's* magazine that contained the famous Betsy McCall paper doll, along with a little pair of scissors. I would cut out the Betsy paper doll and excitedly play until it was time to go home. I always felt extreme joy in my heart at Mrs. Thompson's home. The light of God shone through her loving eyes and her warm heart.

As I reminisced about Mrs. Thompson, I realized that now I wanted to have that same kind of loving, inviting Christian home. I coveted her gift of hospitality and wanted to follow the example she had been to so many as a Sunday school teacher.

I could feel a calling from God to teach a Sunday school class, but He whispered that I had to give up social drinking first. I knew it could become a stumbling block for the youth that I would be teaching, and I wouldn't be setting a good example.

I was under conviction of the Holy Spirit when something dreadful happened. I got a phone call to say that my dear friend Ruth had been killed in a car accident caused by a drunk driver. She was expecting her first baby, but the accident took the life of Ruth and her unborn child. Her husband, Dennis, was seriously injured, but his life was spared. I vividly remember the pain in my heart. I loved Ruth. I kept thinking about her mother and the devastation through which she was walking. Ruth's death was so painful and impacted my life deeply. I realized that my choices in life could adversely affect other people.

In the days and months to follow, I continually thought about the choices the person driving the other car had made. That person made a choice to drink alcohol and get behind the wheel, and now Ruth and her baby were dead. What a tragic decision that person driving the other car made that day, and how he must regret the impact his decisions made on Ruth's family! It made me think how we must search our hearts about choices we make and seek God's face. He will lead us on a path of righteousness to make the right decisions. I could see through this tragic situation that our bad choices can have devastating consequences.

The heart-rending loss of my friend, Ruth, made me really stop and think about my choices. Would the day come when I would drink and regret it? I knew deep inside the answer could be "yes." I asked God to give me the desire to quit, because I couldn't seem to get it on my own.

The Holy Spirit was living in me according to Romans 8:9, 10, and now I had the power to live a more sanctified life in Him. He answered my prayer, and the desire came into my heart by way of an accident in my own life.

It was a hot Sunday afternoon on Memorial Day weekend when my sister Linda and I went to visit her friends in Huntsville, Alabama. We went out in the boat to enjoy the day. Her friend went up to the lake house to get some beer. Linda never really had any interest in drinking, but I still thought it was fun. Her friend was walking down the hill with our beer on a tray, as we were heading toward a rock embankment to pick her up. The motor of the boat was shut off, but we were approaching the rocks a little too fast.

I was in the front of the boat, so I tried to push the boat back when we hit the rock embankment. My right hand and wrist were struck between the boat and the rock wall. Immediately, my hand and wrist began to swell and then turn black and blue. I felt like I was going to pass out, and everything got foggy like cotton balls were over my eyes. The very first thing my eyes saw when my vision returned was the beer on the tray.

Suddenly, I had no interest in drinking a beer. I just wanted to go back home to the ER to have my hand and wrist checked. They were obviously severely broken. X-rays revealed I had three broken bones. The doctor said it was my radius, navicular and lunate. It was a complex break because two of the bones were very small and delicate. They would be difficult to heal, and my cast would have to stay on for three months. He said even when the cast came off at the end of the summer, I might still need to have plates and screws surgically set to make my hand and wrist work properly again.

The technician was instructed to mold the cast from the tips of my fingers up to my shoulder. As I sat there, he told me to position my hand as if I were holding a beer can—not a soda can, a cup or a glass, but a "beer can!" We left the ER that night to go home, and the words kept ringing in my ears: "form your hand like you are holding a beer can." Really? a beer can? Those words rang in my ears over and over.

As I prayed to God in the days that followed the accident, I knew there was something big to be learned. I asked God to show me, and He whispered that it was time for me to give up drinking completely. I sat alone on the sofa in our den and wept because this was not easy. I resisted God and thought of how much I enjoyed a glass of wine on Friday nights. Could one glass lead to two? Could two glasses lead to three? God's Word says in Proverbs 20:1, "Wine is a mocker, strong drink is raging: and whosoever is deceived thereby is not wise." I knew that the temptation of alcohol was strong; however, God's power was stronger. I surrendered and made the decision ***never* to drink any type of alcohol again—ever.** I felt totally convicted, and I knew the conviction was real. I knew I could overcome because victory was mine through Jesus. I felt so loved because He provided my broken arm to stop me from ever desiring to drink again.

I was set free—free from deciding how many drinks I would have at a party, free from ever making a compromised decision influenced by alcohol; and yes, I was free to teach a Sunday school class. I felt my obedience to give up social drinking forever brought blessings to my life and a deep peace in my heart.

Chapter 5

Growing in the Lord

I John 3:22—Whatsoever we ask, we receive of him, because we keep his commandments, and do those things that are pleasing in his sight.

The year following the accident my precious daughter Abby was born. What a blessing! She and Kelly are about four years apart in age. Kelly adored her little sister, and life was good.

I began to understand salvation through faith in what Jesus had done for me. My faith became very personal. I wanted to grow in the Lord. I felt it was possible now because I no longer carried the heavy load of guilt. I could rest in God's forgiveness through the blood of Jesus. This is the thing for which I had longed throughout my whole life.

I was so excited when I was asked to teach a Sunday school class. I accepted, and God began to teach **me** as I taught the children in my class. I was finally truly growing in the Lord. **I still had so much to learn. I knew that the key to security in my life and peace in my heart came from asking God to help me.** I learned that my obedience was very pleasing to Him.

I was at a Wednesday night church service when I experienced the next turning point in my walk with God. On this particular Wednesday night, the ladies of the church gathered for our monthly ladies' prayer meeting in a small classroom where our pastor's wife usually taught her class. There were about fifteen of us in attendance. It was a very intimate group, and we began to share our prayer requests.

Our pastor's wife, Mrs. Nancy, began to cry profusely. She said she needed to confess something. I thought, "Wow, she must have done something really terrible to cry like that." She regained her composure and confessed that she had not been praying like she should. I thought to myself, "Go on. Tell us about your sin," but that was it! I sat there thinking that she had to be kidding. She was that upset because she didn't pray enough?

I was moved by her sincerity and brokenness over what I thought to be a small thing—not taking more time to pray. I thought of my own life at age twenty-eight and wished that my biggest conviction by the Holy Spirit was that I was not praying enough. I sat very still and looked deep into my own heart, and God helped me to realize that I was knee-deep in sin.

I was a lot like my friends, so I thought I was an okay person. However, **Mrs. Nancy said never to compare yourself to your friends; compare yourself to Jesus.** If you follow the example of the world, you will be like the world. Comparison can soothe us, but it can also deceive us. It can make us feel justified with sinful actions. On the other hand, comparison can dishearten us when we feel others are doing better than us. Either way, it is inaccurate and deceiving. Satan loves it when we compare ourselves to others.

I asked God to change me that very night. I asked God to help me look to Him, and not at others. I asked Him to reveal sin in my life and to help me overcome it. I claimed the Scripture "greater is he that is in you, than he that is in the world" (I John 4:4).

God immediately began to do His work in my heart, and this has continued throughout the years. He took the sin in my life and began to peel away the layers.

The Lord didn't reveal to me all of my shortcomings at one time. I think I would have become too discouraged. God has shown me day by day, month by month, the things that are not pleasing to Him; and He has planted my feet on higher ground. In this life I will never attain a place of perfection; however, I pray for a pure and clean heart that wants to please Him.

Over time, I have prayed asking God to help me in every area of my life. He has revealed so many things to me and provided beyond what I could have ever imagined. **Now I, like Mrs. Nancy, can hunger continually to be improving my prayer life and my daily Bible study, because these are the keys to having the power and the peace of the Lord.**

Mrs. Nancy taught us that once we have invited Jesus into our hearts, He has promised in His Word that He will never leave us or forsake us. I thank the Lord for the privilege of prayer and that God keeps His promises. I began to be much more aware of God's presence and of His working on my behalf. Though I didn't know it, huge struggles were to be in my future but I knew Jesus was with me and would carry me through whatever lay ahead. I learned to trust Him more through faith by spending quiet time alone with Him. I began to understand better how to receive His acceptance and forgiveness; and in turn, I released myself from yesterday's mistakes and had the courage to face the future.

Chapter 6

Walking Humbly

James 4:6—God resisteth the proud, but giveth grace unto the humble.

God's timing is always perfect. He had worked in my life and was preparing me for the difficult road just ahead. Daddy had suffered so much from his heart attacks, an aortic aneurism and congestive heart failure. I watched as my strong father's health deteriorated and he got weaker and weaker. He was only sixty-two when he passed away. It was such a sad time for all of us. We were all heartbroken.

In the first year that followed his death, I thought about him every day. Coping with tragedy is difficult, but a positive perspective from the Lord carried me through. He was so faithful through this tough time in my life. The trials we endure can introduce us to our own strengths. There were things that I learned from Daddy's life and death. I was only thirty years old, and I still had so many things to learn about life.

I spent a lot of time reminiscing about what kind of person my daddy was. He was such a good man, but he had some insecurities because he had spent most of his life without the love and care of his mother. She died of breast cancer when he was nine years old. She left behind six young children and a grieving husband. My grandfather remarried and continued to be a devoted father to his children, but the kind of mother love we all crave ended for Daddy when he was nine.

I suppose Daddy was always extremely thankful for everything because he had been given so little. He appreciated every little thing in life and taught us to do the same. He loved tulips and hyacinths in the spring, yellow roses in full bloom and catching fish to fry for supper in the summer, bonfires at the river in the fall, and playing Santa Claus at Christmas. My daddy was a good man. He inspired me to appreciate and **focus on the good things in my life.**

My mother needed her children to step up and help her through the days after Dad's death. We all were privileged to do that. Mama was always such a humble person, and I believe God honored her as she humbly walked with Him.

I wanted to be humble like Mama, but it was difficult for me to identify all the manifestations of pride in my life. It comes in so many forms, all of which are displeasing to our Heavenly Father. Jesus was so humble, and He set a perfect example for us.

One morning as I was doing my Bible study, God revealed to me something about myself. As I sat in my chair and read James, chapter 4, I read verse 6 over and over again. James 4:6 tells us that God resists the proud but gives grace unto the humble. I thought of Mama's humble spirit as I pondered the verse, and I realized something was not exactly right in my heart. The spotlight of God's Word shone into a corner of my heart. I was like an ungrateful child who was given so much, yet wanted credit as if His gifts were my own doing. I was somewhat insecure, like Daddy, because I wanted credit for the things I did. My mother never wanted credit for anything nor did she want to be in the spotlight. I needed to make some changes.

I got on my knees and asked God not to resist me due to my pride. He removed Satan's blinders from my eyes and allowed me to see the sin of pride in my life the way He saw it. It was at that moment I realized pride was a stronghold and I confessed it before God. I felt very emotional because it was difficult to admit how much I had sugarcoated the awful sin of pride.

Pride had given me a hunger for recognition and honor from other people. It had kept me from totally knowing and accepting myself. **I was trying so hard to be all I could be until I realized God was telling me just to be myself, my best self, for Him and for His glory.** I changed deep inside that morning and knew it was another layer that God was peeling off me.

At this turning point in my life, I knew I didn't have to **perform**; I had to **obey**. My heart belonged to God, but I wondered if I really knew His heart. I began to ask Him to help me to know Him better. This greater respect for God's authority brought with it a more willing attitude to be a servant to Him and others.

> *"He hath shewed thee, O man, what is good; and what doth the LORD require of thee, but to do justly, and to love mercy, and to walk humbly with thy God?"*—Micah 6:8.

I found deeper peace in my life, because it was not about me anymore; it was about my love, respect and obedience to God. God's Word had spoken to me about how Satan had used pride to keep me from fully obeying God and keeping His commandments. Previously I had thought pride was a small thing; then I learned that God views it as sin. I

50

realized my lack of humility could be the root and foundation on which other sin had grown.

Admitting my helplessness was one of the best prayers I ever prayed. I suddenly felt like a pressure valve had been released in my life because His love and my desire to obey with humility brought forth perfect peace in my heart. **The revelation of the sin of pride led to an obedience that was key in hearing from God.** I humbled myself and began to trust that God is always good and always right.

I am amazed at how Satan keeps us from seeing how pride prevents us from experiencing the Lord's blessings. We deceive ourselves when we have not been humbled. Pride keeps us from hearing the voice of God.

It doesn't stop there. Pride is something with which we must deal on a daily basis. Our flesh is always fighting to reign over our spirits.

We all sin. First John 1:8 says, "If we say that we have no sin, we deceive ourselves, and the truth is not in us." Satan tells us we are good once we become Christians. This is a trap we fall into when we don't display any obvious sin and we think we are living right. First Corinthians 3:3 tells us about sins in our hearts that can't be seen by others. This is why we need to search our hearts daily. The Holy Spirit can reveal our sin to us when we are very still and listening.

Proverbs 6:16–19 says there are some things that God actually **hates** and they are an abomination to Him. The very first thing the Bible says He hates is a proud look. It blinds us from giving Him the honor and glory for the simple things we take for granted, like our daily provisions. **I realized that I should humble myself daily and with thanksgiving in my heart depend on Him for everything.** Our humble faith and obedience can open the door to ask Him for everything we need. **Obedience brings blessings**.

This was the beginning of learning how better to hear the voice of God and respond with obedience.

Chapter 7

The Wounded Lamb

John 10:27—My sheep hear my voice, and I know them, and they follow me.

All of humanity share the common thread that we have sinned; however, God is in the business of restoring lives and offering us hope in our most difficult times. My life has had disappointing times. My husband, Eddie, and I divorced after seventeen years of marriage, and it was difficult for me and my daughters. I had to pick up the pieces, and the Lord provided everything I needed during those hard times.

He provided forgiveness, and He made full provision for our every need. He gradually mended our lives and our hearts. God calmed the chaos in my family as Christian friends prayed for us. Sometimes life is just hard. **It got better when I gave up the idea that the past should have been different and just asked The Lord to meet me right where I was at that moment.** He did just that! Being a Christian and serving the Lord are what kept me focused and solvent.

I once heard that people are about as happy as they make their minds up to be. My mind was made up to be happy because I had the joy of the Lord deep in my heart. I found so much happiness in taking care of my daughters. I enjoyed everything about them. They had lots of friends. It was our regular routine to have five or six of their friends over every Friday night to play and spend the night. This would be followed by a big country breakfast I would prepare for them on Saturday mornings. I spent my time trying to be the best mother I could be for Kelly and Abby. Happiness was always around us, but it was up to us to look for it. I looked for it and found it in God and my two precious daughters. I was so blessed!

My circumstances were not what I had dreamed, but God worked in mysterious ways. Satan, the enemy, was trying to rob me of my calling from God; and I could not allow my past to define me. I stayed close to the Lord, but I struggled in many ways. I really felt it was in this valley that there were times I was in its depths, but God pulled me out as only He can. He was always good and He was always right.

About two years after the divorce, I was visiting my dear friend, Beth Scott, at St. Thomas Hospital in Nashville. I had just returned home from a much needed vacation with my dear friend, Debbie. While I was away on vacation, Beth had a serious heart attack at only thirty-four years of age. Upon my return, I went to the hospital and joined her mother at her bedside. During my visit, one of her friends, Herbert Woodard, came in to visit her also. He seemed very nice; however, I didn't take much notice of him at that moment because I was so upset about Beth. I left her room with a heavy heart, praying for her complete recovery.

That evening Beth called me and said Herbert had visited for a while. Once he was sure she was okay, he asked her about me. She told him I was single and about our close friendship. He asked for my phone number. She hesitantly gave it to him. I told her that it was fine and I was glad she did. She spoke very highly of him and said she had known him for a long time. She said he was divorced and had one daughter about Abby's age.

He called me the following Sunday afternoon and asked if I would have dinner with him on Monday evening. I accepted, but explained he would have to come to my house since I already had plans to grill for Kelly's French Club cookout. He arrived to find about thirty-five kids at my house. I was so impressed when Herbert came in and began helping me. He started flipping burgers on the grill and then helped with the cleanup. We talked and laughed like I had known him all of my life. I knew this man was someone very special. At the end of the evening, he held my hand and my heart whispered that he was "the one" for me.

We were so comfortable with each other. I couldn't stop thinking about him. The following weekend, he asked me to go fishing. I got up at 5:00 a.m. and met him at the boat dock. I love to fish, so I was excited to get started. It was a very sunny day, but it was really a bit too windy to be fishing. He spent most of the day fighting the wind with his trolling motor so that I could keep casting. At the end of the day, I had landed a pretty good-sized smallmouth and a nice largemouth bass. It was the best day ever and my heart was full! Herbert later told his sister, Wanda, that he decided that day I was "the one" for him.

Herbert's brother, Ronnie, and sister-in-law, Nancie, had led him to the Lord three years prior to our meeting. They had prayed and asked God to bring a Christian woman into his life. When I met them, they told me I was an answer to their prayers. I knew Herbert was sent to me by the Lord. After my salvation, Herbert and my children are best things that ever happened to me in my life.

We fell in love immediately and talked every day. Herbert was everything I could have ever asked for. I was so happy. On a cold December night, he said when he looked into his heart, he could only see me—forever. He got on one knee and looked at me with his beautiful eyes and asked me to marry him. I said yes, and we were so excited about the idea of spending our lives together.

We went to my mom's house to tell her. The three of us were having coffee at her kitchen table, and I shared our good news. Without saying a single word in reply, she got up from her chair and left the room. I told Herbert not to worry because she's not very expressive, but even I thought that was a little strange.

Moments later she came back in and sat down. She lifted her hands to the table and handed Herbert my daddy's wedding band. She said, "Herbert, Raymond would want you to have this ring." I could hardly believe such a sweet, sentimental thing was coming from my mama. Herbert was so moved. He thanked her and told her that he was very honored. I couldn't imagine what came next. She looked at me and slipped her wedding band from her ring finger and handed it to me. "I want you to have mine, Rita," she said. I started crying and knew God was in this engagement. Mama gave us her blessings, and there were no words to describe how I knew God had answered all our prayers. We were married the next year.

Herbert and I shared God's miracle of marriage. Knowing God truly joined us together, we became one flesh according to Genesis 2:24. We thanked the Lord for being the God of second chances who forgives us and cleanses us from all unrighteousness (I John 1:9).

That was in 1994, and God has taught us so much through our years together. I thank God often for the good, strong man He sent me that day in Beth's coronary care hospital room. God has given us a good life in a wonderful, old colonial home in the country with fifteen acres. We have been here for over twenty years, and we love it. It takes more than a house to make a home; it's the people that share it. God has used our home to be a refuge for missionaries. It has been a place for others to have weddings and celebrations of all kinds. Our home is the place where we host the annual family Easter egg hunt, and we celebrate Christ's resurrection. We have shared many wonderful times here at our home that we call Fair Haven. However, life is not always full of fun. We have experienced times of pain and sadness, as most families do, but God has been faithful through them all. Our family experienced turmoil in the late nineties and many things changed in our family dynamics. Painful changes. Life was hard.

Herbert and I both knew that our joy didn't come from the world and the circumstances life brought. It came from faith in God. It was when we turned our eyes to the Word of God that our hearts truly mended from pains of the past and we flourished.

As we allowed the Holy Spirit to work in our hearts, we found incomparable, overcoming power. His strength is made perfect in our weakness. We served God together as we continued to ask Him for His supernatural power to help us to become what He wanted us to be.

In 2003 we began searching for a new church home in which to get grounded again. What a hectic time in my life; but at the same time such a wonderment at God moving the pieces of my life to fit his plan!

I told my niece, Brandy, how I felt, and she invited us to visit her Sunday school class the next Sunday. We took her up on it and loved it. We went back to her church that evening and Wednesday night and joined the church the next Sunday. The Lord had indeed led us to this wonderful church. We were growing spiritually together.

This was a large church. I didn't jump right in and look for ways to serve. I think God actually brought us to this church to provide support for the very difficult days that were just ahead of us. Only two months after we joined the church, He changed my life with a cancer diagnosis. I felt like a little lost lamb, helpless and frightened.

When I think of how I felt at that time of my life, I am reminded of our recent trip to Europe. One of the most memorable things happened while we were in Sicily. We were on a bus tour traveling across the countryside, and I noticed that there were a lot of sheep in the fields. It appeared the Sicilians raise sheep in the way we raise cattle and horses in Tennessee.

I kept noticing the sheep grazing in the beautiful pastures; then as we rounded a curve, my eyes captured a sight I had never seen before. A shepherd, in the midst of a lush green pasture, was ambling up a rolling hill with his sheep snuggly around him. I couldn't take my eyes off this scene. The beautiful countryside was so vast, and the shepherd and his flock were a sight to behold. As they disappeared out of view, I couldn't stop thinking about what I had just seen. I was reminded of what Jesus Christ says in John 10:14: "I am the good shepherd, and know my sheep." He goes on to say in verse 27, "My sheep hear my voice, and I know them, and they follow me."

The Lord wants intimate communication with His people like a shepherd with his sheep. He wants us to stay close to Him and know His voice when He speaks. We can petition Him and thank Him in prayer. This is how we communicate with Him; He speaks to us through His Word and through the "still small voice" of the Holy Spirit in the sacred places in our hearts.

To have God's power in our lives, we need to have a personal relationship with Jesus. God uses the Bible and prayer as tools to guide us. He really wants to do good works in and through our lives. If we make a commitment to obey Him and humble ourselves, we will begin to hear His voice more clearly. We may choose to obey or not to obey.

When we choose not to obey, we are like a lamb that goes astray and wanders off alone. (A wandering sheep symbolizes any one of us when we continue to be disobedient to God's perfect will.) The shepherd may seek out the errant lamb and dislocate its leg in an attempt to protect it. He will carry it back to the flock on his shoulders, and the lamb will continue to be carried by the shepherd while its leg is healing. As the leg mends, the lamb will hear the voice of the shepherd, and it will become a very familiar voice. Once the lamb is healed, it will trust and faithfully follow close by the shepherd.

I thought about what we had seen on that hillside in Sicily, and I pondered the analogy of the little lamb. I began to reminisce about the healing God was to bring about in my own life. **I was that lamb!**

It is our season of pain that seems to make us stop to hear the voice of our Shepherd. This is when God picks us up and tenderly carries us if we let Him. I knew that I wanted Him to pick me up and carry me. I also knew that the more fully I set my heart on listening, the more clearly I would hear His voice. This was definitely a time I needed to hear His voice—loud and clear. He wanted me once again to hear Him and truly experience His power, holiness and tender mercies. The closer I got to Him, the more I was humbled and in awe of Him.

Chapter 8

Bearing New Fruits

*Luke 13:9—And if it bear fruit,
well: and if not, then after that
thou shall cut it down.*

It was a beautiful Monday morning in May of 2003. The day began with a routine mammogram. I felt great when I was told everything looked good. As I was getting into my car to leave, the technician came out and asked me to come back in to talk to the doctor. The pathologist met with me immediately and said there was a spot deep in my chest wall that was showing up, and he referred me to a breast center in Nashville, Tennessee.

I left the Murfreesboro Imaging Center and went to the St. Thomas Breast Center to have a more extensive mammogram. I was there for a couple of hours doing tests, when the doctor determined the spot must be biopsied. The doctor was so concerned that she decided to use her lunch break to perform my biopsy right then. She was very compassionate and kind. I was so thankful for her.

I left that office knowing I would have confirmed results within forty-eight hours. The results would let me know if I had breast cancer.

II Timothy 1:7 tells us that God has not given us the spirit of fear, but of power, love and a sound mind. I claimed this Scripture and asked God to take away my fear. I realized that it was up to me to claim the promises of God no matter what the test results revealed.

My grandmother was stricken with breast cancer and died at the young age of thirty-six. She left behind six small children, one of whom was my father. Would I too have a malignant tumor that would cost me my life? I began to seek God's face. He reassured me I could trust Him for perfect peace. He is my Father, and I could once again feel His actual presence. Somehow I knew in my heart that I had cancer, and He began to prepare me emotionally for the news.

The forty-eight hours finally passed. I was at my mother's home on Wednesday morning when the phone call came. It was a very difficult conversation.

The nurse said, "Mrs. Woodard, I am sorry to tell you that the tumor in your breast is malignant. Would you be available to come in to the office this afternoon for us to provide details and explain your options?"

I agreed and thanked her for calling.

I hung up the phone and then quietly turned to my mama and told her that I had breast cancer. I wasn't sure how she would respond. Small tears began to run down my precious mama's cheeks.

What a blessing from the Lord that my mother expressed her love in such a meaningful, heartfelt way. My mother was not very expressive or affectionate. She loved deeply; however, she usually demonstrated it by acts of service, not by words of affirmation or physical affection. This time was very different. She hugged me and she actually began to cry. She was crying for me. I will never forget that special moment in time that brought such indescribable comfort.

I felt deeply loved because I had only seen her cry twice in my whole life. She cried when her brother, Homer, died and again when my father died. I knew she loved them both very much; so the fact that she was so emotional made me feel so loved.

I called my husband, and he came to pick me up immediately. We went directly to Nashville to see the doctor. He said the cancer needed to be removed surgically as soon as possible. I wanted to get it out of my body as soon as I could.

Fortunately, the surgeon was also able to meet with us that same afternoon at three o'clock. We decided to have the surgery on Friday morning, and I considered it a blessing that it could be scheduled that soon.

I had found out on Monday that I might have breast cancer, it had been confirmed on Wednesday, and I was scheduled to have surgery on Friday. This difficult, emotional week was when I became the lamb on Jesus' shoulders as we began our long journey. The Lord revealed His strength in my weakness.

It was time to demonstrate my faith because one of life's testing times had come. I had talked the talk, and now it was time to walk the walk. It was up to me to exercise my faith and accept whatever was ahead, knowing it would be for my good and for God's glory. My husband agreed with me that God was in control, yet I could feel that his heart was extremely heavy.

My precious family and close friends were with me when Friday morning finally came. The surgery was successful and without complications. The surgeon said that the cancer was complex and aggressive. The tumor was typed as invasive ductal cell carcinoma. It was considered very aggressive because it was classified as a triple-negative cancer. This type carries a high risk of relapse and is complicated to treat. I began the series of thirty-two radiation treatments the next week.

A common question people have when diagnosed with cancer is "Why?" If God had a lesson for me in this, I didn't want to miss it. God answered my "why?" when He led me to the story of the fruitless fig tree in Luke 13:6–9:

"He [Jesus] *spake also this parable; A certain man had a fig tree planted in his vineyard; and he came and sought fruit thereon, and found none. Then said he unto the dresser of his vineyard, Behold, these three years I come seeking fruit on this fig tree, and find none: cut it down; why cumbereth it the ground? And he answering said unto him, Lord, let it alone this year also, till I shall dig about it, and dung it: And if it bear fruit, well: and if not, then after that thou shall cut it down."*

As I read the parable of the fruitless fig tree, God spoke to my heart and revealed to me that this was what I had become in the last three years due to my busy schedule. I had allowed my heavy workload and activities to keep me from being fruitful for the Lord. I knew that I needed my life to be fruitful, and Jesus was ready to "dig and dung" my heart. I needed the hardened ground around my heart to be loosened and fertilized with time to read my Bible and pray. I needed to make time in my day again for the Lord. My life needed to bear fruit once more. Like that fruitless fig tree, I felt like I was going to have a second chance.

After reading the fig tree Scripture, I knew why God had allowed me to walk through this valley. I believed He would give me another chance.

I asked God what I should do to be fruitful for Him. He laid it on my heart to begin a ministry where I should invite ladies into my home for "Fruitful Ladies" dinners. I would prepare dinner, and each lady would share what she does to serve God. My mission was to thank them and to encourage them to keep on "keeping on" for the glory of God. As Christians, we need to encourage each other to keep doing God's work.

Too many Christians have given up serving the Lord and are dropping out of good churches. The world is offering more and more fun things to do on the Lord's day. God wants us to encourage one another. Through breast cancer, I knew God had given me the gift of encouragement.

My spiritual gift had always been hospitality, but now I was confident that He had given me a second gift—encouragement. I knew it was time to start using both gifts. I continued to ask God what else I could do and He answered as I sat in a Wednesday night church service. He led me to I Corinthians 15:57, 58. This scripture reassures us that our labor is not in vain in the Lord. I envisioned these two verses painted on the wall around the ceiling of one of our bedrooms in the upstairs of our house. This is not my life verse, but it is encouraging to every believer.

Then I began to think we could use our upstairs bedrooms to house missionaries and encourage them to keep on "keeping on" for the Lord. It was all coming together to help me become more fruitful and use my gifts. I called my oldest brother, Danny, and he painted that Scripture around the wall for us. He was an artist and a sign painter by profession. His work turned out beautifully, and the Scripture text fit in the space perfectly.

The missionaries began to come to us through some of the local Baptist churches in our city. We remodeled our upstairs bathrooms to make our accommodations the best they could be for our guests. We love our missionary guests as we serve them as unto the Lord.

It is such a blessing to share our home with God's people. We want to provide them rest and refreshment in hopes that our encouragement will help them as they serve God.

One missionary couple, Darrell and Joanie, stayed with us and got emotional when they saw the

Scripture on the wall because their ministry was based on it. They felt God's love through it. I was blessed when Joanie left me the book that she wrote which contains a quote from a lady named Louise who had housed them on a mission trip. Louise said, *"One day we will be able to sing and enjoy Heaven for all of eternity. But it is only here on earth that we can love, serve and minister one to another **as unto the Lord**."*

I began to be sensitive to ways I could serve and minister to others. **One thing that the Lord taught me during this time was that little is much when He is in it.** Sometimes we wait until we can do something big for God. He showed me it is quite the contrary. I learned to listen more closely for His voice and to obey when He speaks to my heart about the little things. He can use our smallest gesture of kindness to bring glory to Him. When we ask God to show us what He wants us to do for others, He will whisper the sweetest things for us to do. We must listen closely. I thank Him for those whispers. They light my path to show me ways to be more fruitful for Him.

I thought my "fruitful" acts were *showing* others God's love, but He had much more for me to learn. He also wanted me to *tell* others of His power.

What a blessing it was to know that God had indeed healed me and carried me through the terror of it all; however, up to this point, I had not shared my experience with many people. I had tried to have a positive attitude and had started *doing fruitful things*, but I had not really *told* or *shared* with others the power God truly has to heal completely.

I should have been more vocal in giving Him the glory. More experiences were in store in my future to move me up to higher ground. Some of the experiences would be pleasant, but some would be extremely difficult. I was surely going to need God's power to navigate through the biggest challenge of my life ahead.

Chapter 9

Walking on Top
of the Valley

*Philippians 1:20, 21—...Christ
shall be magnified in my body,
whether it be by life, or by
death. For to me to live is
Christ, and to die is gain.*

In May 2004, only one year after being diagnosed
with breast cancer, God began the next chapter in my
life. It started with an impression deep in my spirit
that something was badly wrong with regard to my
health. I tried to describe the feeling to my friends,
Kim Gaither and Becky Johnson. I expressed my
concern and attempted to define the premonition, but

it was indescribable. I told them that I felt like there was something seriously wrong inside me that might cause me to die. I explained that I felt like either I was going to have a heart attack or possibly cancer had taken over my body...again. It was just a totally weird, urgent feeling that I couldn't explain. They told me to trust my feelings and suggested that I go to the doctor to get checked out.

I made an appointment with a cardiologist, and he said that my heart was healthy. I felt relieved about that, but a gnawing inside my spirit kept telling me that something was wrong. A lack of peace plays a big part in learning to hear God's voice. The absence of peace in my heart told me to listen closely to what He wanted to say to me. I was in turmoil as the feeling that cancer was taking over my body would not leave me. I needed to see a doctor. I just knew I must see one very soon. I felt a little lost because my gynecologist, Dr. LaRoche, whom I adored and had seen most of my adult life, was no longer taking my insurance. I decided to go to Nashville to see a new doctor. We discussed my medical history, and I explained the feelings I was having in as much detail as possible. I stressed to her my concerns and that I wanted to have a CT scan to be sure I was okay, but she insisted that I was being overanxious and my insurance wouldn't cover it anyway.

That was a moment when a doctor, the expert, told me something and I was expected to accept it, say "thank you," and go home. I couldn't. I asked her to submit a request to see if insurance would possibly cover it, but she never followed through. I knew she thought she was right, but my suspicion was much different from hers. I had to choose to be submissive and bow to her authority or to be a no-nonsense survivor who would own my health.

My previous doctor had a sign that hung in the patients' exam room that said **Own Your Health.** She said to always trust your spirit to know how you feel.

I mustered up my confidence, and as politely as possible, I insisted that my new doctor do tests of some kind to help me understand why I was having misgivings about my health. I made several visits to her office over the course of six months. She did some ultrasounds and various tests and concluded that she couldn't find anything of consequence amiss. Then she opted to do a D&C, which was a minor surgical procedure, to be sure everything was all right. She reassured me that I was fine and everything looked okay.

I couldn't get peace in my heart about her conclusions. I had seven months of terrible feelings that something was badly wrong with me. I wanted desperately to believe my doctor, but I couldn't.

Late one Thursday afternoon in September of 2004, I was meeting with a client when an overwhelming urge overcame me to go to my doctor's office and insist on a CT scan. I couldn't focus on our meeting and asked if I could reschedule. The client agreed.

With my heart pounding, I left the meeting and went straight to my doctor's office without an appointment. I walked in and told the receptionist that I must see the doctor. Since I had had the recent surgical procedure, she agreed to get me in right away, thinking that there might have been complications. I explained to the doctor there were no complications but something wasn't right and, with urgency, I insisted on a CT scan. She said that I couldn't just walk in and insist on a scan. I began to cry uncontrollably and begged her to do one because I knew that something was terribly wrong with me. She said the only way that she could order it was for me to be admitted to the hospital. I pleaded with her to admit me; and with exasperation, undoubtedly thinking I was some kind of a nut, she finally agreed to it. She filled out the paperwork to have me admitted as an emergency patient.

I have to admit, it felt very strange lying on the hospital bed with nothing apparently wrong with me—no pain, no injury and no real symptoms. I didn't have to have a medical degree to know that there was something terribly wrong inside my body. I was not afraid to question my doctor's authority because I felt confident that I was following the authority of the Holy Spirit that lives in me. I had to stand up for myself, no matter how uncomfortable it felt. God had given me intelligence to think for myself and trust my judgment. I knew He was giving the orders here and I had to obey.

My husband, Herbert, and my daughters Kelly and Abby all rushed to be with me. I am pretty sure they thought I had lost my mind. I was "just fine" lying on the hospital bed. We talked and visited until bedtime, and then they all went home.

A couple of hours later, close to midnight, the word came that the CT scan was approved by insurance. At 2:00 a.m. they rolled me out for the emergency scan. I felt so happy to be getting the scan so I could be sure of what was going on inside me.

A few short hours later, at 7:00 a.m., my doctor walked into my room with a very long face. With all of her arrogance left behind, she looked at the floor as she said, "Well, you were right. There is something very serious going on with you, Rita. The scan shows a tumor in your pelvic area, and it appears that you have ovarian cancer. Also, I think that it may be at a very advanced stage, so we will need to do another test called a PET scan. I am turning your case over to our specialist who is a gynecological oncologist. He has just ordered the radioactive dye for the test, and we will have it done first thing on Monday morning at Vanderbilt Medical Center."

I said, "Thank you." That is all I could say. She looked down, then turned and walked away.

God was present in the valley with me at that very moment, just as He has been with me on all of my mountaintops. He is Lord over both of them. I felt His very real presence at that moment. I called Herbert. He came to be with me immediately. I called my family and then I called my friend Becky. She said, "It is crazy how you knew something was terribly wrong. It had to be the Holy Spirit impressing it on your heart." She told Kim, and they prayed for me. They are both faithful friends and powerful prayer warriors.

As a matter of fact, when I think of the sad morning I learned of the cancer, thoughts of the people who lifted me up in prayer flood my soul. So many people began praying for my healing. Many reached out to me to let me know how much they were praying. Prayer is the greatest privilege of being a Christian. Being the recipient of other people's prayers proved to be one of my greatest blessings during this difficult time.

With the news of ovarian cancer, I was not sure what God wanted me to learn but, without delay, I began to ask Him to show me. I believe He always has a lesson for me in my valleys and I didn't want to miss this one.

Monday morning finally came, and I went in for the PET scan. The sweet technician came in and administered the radioactive dye and said that I had to lie completely still for an hour. She said that the dye would go to any cancerous tumor in my body and when they scanned me, it would light up. I vividly remembered lying totally still, and I thought of the Scripture, Psalm 46:10, "Be still, and know that I am God."

All of my thoughts began to focus on God and His power. God had a plan. He used the "still" time to prepare me for the news that I was about to receive. He moved in my heart in a big way to reassure me that He was going to carry me as a shepherd carries a little, wounded lamb. He reassured me that He was in control and I could totally trust Him. I felt amazingly calm and at perfect peace.

Wednesday afternoon I got the call from my doctor while driving home. The report was not good. He used the word "treacherous" to describe it. My doctor spoke the words compassionately as he strongly emphasized the severity of the cancer.

Once I got home, I walked to the riding arena beside our barn. I watched my husband as he loped gentle circles on his horse. Herbert, a man I love so completely, rode beautifully as he went round and round. He sat tall in the saddle. Little did I know how broken my tall, strong cowboy would be with my news. He dismounted when he saw me, and tied his horse to the fence. He walked up to me, and we began to talk. I looked into his eyes as I told him the doctor had explained we needed to prepare ourselves for the worst.

He said, "I don't want to live without you Rita." With broken hearts, together we stood and cried. It was then, somehow and very suddenly that I felt comfort. I can't explain it, but I have never felt so loved. It was as though God reached down from Heaven with both arms and wrapped them around us.

We got up early Thursday morning to go to the doctor to discuss the test results. God had truly prepared me for them, and they were really bad. In fact, it was worse than bad, it was about the worst news I could have gotten.

The adenocarcinoma had spread from my ovary to my liver. There was a metastasized tumor showing up by my liver and it was quite large. My oncologist hung his head and he explained the entire situation in great detail. My mind was reeling. I wanted to think positive and look on the bright side. The problem was that he wasn't really giving us any encouraging information at this point.

He said that I would need surgery immediately and it would require two separate surgeons. One would be the gynecological oncologist specialist. He would perform the complete hysterectomy to remove the cancer in my pelvic area, and the other surgeon would perform the surgery in my abdomen to remove the malignant tumor by my liver. God whispered to me to trust Him and, though I was hearing terrible news, I felt peace.

In light of this news on that Thursday morning, my husband asked if we should cancel our trip to a couples retreat where we had planned to go that evening. Our church had planned the annual couples retreat and we were very excited about going. I felt like we should go because it would be good for us to be with Christian friends during this difficult time.

The retreat was being held at a state park, and it was just what we needed. The fall weather was beautiful. We could see God's handiwork in the gorgeous gold, orange and red leaves. The autumn colors were at their peak, and there was a crisp chill in the air. As we all sat around a big, crackling bonfire on that Thursday evening after our dinner, people began to share their testimonies of what God had done in their lives. Some told about His power and His faithfulness in their lives, while others shared their prayer requests for their burdens.

As I listened to them share, I tried to process my own thoughts: "How do I share that I am sitting here pondering songs to be sung at my funeral?" I tried to wrap my mind around what it actually means to get my house in order. I was thinking that I was probably not going to live much longer and I wondered what that really meant. How long did I have?

As the fire crackled and I felt its warmth, the Holy Spirit prompted me to be brave, and share what the doctor had told us that morning. I explained about the aggressive breast cancer that I had the previous year and said that I now had advanced ovarian cancer with a metastatic tumor by my liver.

I told them that I had been sitting around the fire partially listening to them, and partially planning my funeral. I had been thinking about how my death would affect Herbert, our precious girls and their families. I went on to share how God had given me peace and that He would carry me through.

Herbert had tears running down his cheeks as his heart was breaking. Our love is so deep. We truly are one flesh through the miracle of marriage. It was hard for me to imagine what **he** must have been feeling. I only know that my strong man was brokenhearted and distraught. He trusted the Lord and tried to be positive and encouraging, but I could feel his deep, unspoken pain.

As our friends sat around the campfire listening to me speak, they were moved to pray for me and they committed to pray for us as we continued on the long journey ahead. Our dear friends, Frank and Doris Todd, shared that they would be our prayer partners and would lift us up to the Lord every day. It meant the world to me, and reminded me that it is so important to encourage the people God lays on your heart. I was glad we made the decision to go to the retreat, even in light of the heavy burden we brought with us. God used others to encourage us, and offer hope when we needed it most.

Never underestimate the power of your kind gestures and encouraging words. First Thessalonians 5:11 tells us to comfort and encourage one another. Part of being a Christian is taking your eyes off yourself and offering comfort to others. We never know how much it helps until we are the one in need. The relationships we develop with others are actually a reflection of who we are. Our relationship with Jesus is the foundation for all the other connections we make with people. Having a close, personal relationship with the Lord is the model for the relationships we have with others.

The next week we met with the gynecological oncologist surgeon, who was a specialist for cancer patients at a hospital in Nashville. He agreed to perform the hysterectomy and was committed to doing all he could to get all of the cancer. The same day, we met with the general surgeon who would remove the malignant tumor from my liver. He said the scan showed the tumor was large.

Both surgeons agreed that I would have both surgeries the next Monday morning. They would work together and perform both surgeries while I was under the anesthesia. I would be under for an extended time period, but they agreed it would be best.

Every woman with ovarian cancer is different, and the specific characteristics of each condition determines how the doctors manage it.

My doctor told me it was difficult to remove advanced ovarian cancer completely and the chemotherapy would be unable to eradicate all of the remaining cancer. He felt the surgeries and platinum-based chemotherapy could possibly help to prolong the time before possible cancer recurrence and improve my chances for survival. I was totally confident in my surgeons and my oncologist, however, my greatest confidence was in the power of Jesus Christ, my Saviour. I knew this had passed through the hand of God, and I trusted Him regardless of the outcome. I knew my life was aligned with God's plan. I felt comfort and reassurance from Him that words cannot describe.

I claimed the promises of God when Monday morning arrived. As I was rolled into surgery, Herbert was by my side. It also warmed my heart that Pastor Norris came to pray with me. A good pastor and church family are an encouraging support group as we walk with Christ. I shared with him that I was not afraid and I totally trusted that God was in control of the outcome.

It was a very long day for my family and close friends. They were all praying for me. The surgeries were finally over and they went smoothly.

My recovery in the hospital was going as planned and it was late in the evening of the fifth day when the nurse came in and said we could go home that night or stay one more day. Herbert and I really wanted to go home, so we opted for leaving that evening. It was a very cold winter night with temperatures dipping into the twenties. We couldn't wait to get to our warm, comfy home, but we were shocked when we walked in because it was freezing cold! Our central heat unit had quit. I was a bit nauseous from the car ride home and in severe pain.

Herbert realized that I couldn't get relief from my pain because the nurse forgot to send home the prescription for pain meds. He wrapped me in our electric blanket to sleep. I lay on the recliner, finally got warm and went to sleep. It was a miserable night, but thankfully God provided wonderful help the next day.

My sister-in-law, Arlene, drove to Nashville to pick up the prescription for pain medicine since it could not be called in or faxed. She has always been like a sister to me and has such a precious, servant's heart. Her daughter, my niece, Tracy, is a nurse practitioner. She spent the whole day taking care of me. My incisions were massive, and I was in terrible pain: she was like an angel.

Thankfully, we were able to get our heating unit replaced that day. I was extremely appreciative of all the provisions the Lord made for us that day. What a wonderful blessing to have caring family members who were there for us!

I spent the next week recovering and preparing myself emotionally for chemotherapy. Once advanced ovarian cancer has metastasized, the cancer cells may spread quickly and form new tumors in other vital organs. It was vital to begin chemotherapy as soon as possible. My body was in a pitiful state due to all of the radiation and surgeries I had been through the previous year, but I was determined to begin the chemo the next week and start my fight against this terrible disease.

My first treatment was to be a totally new experience for me. I had to take steroid shots before the treatment to help avoid adverse reactions to the chemo. The shots totally "wired" me, so I didn't sleep a wink. I became anxious as the unknown crept into my mind. On the way to my first treatment, I began to cry. Herbert was driving and he said he shared my emotions. Many people don't realize the pain that a spouse feels as their loved one undergoes the trials of cancer. He was so compassionate and such a precious blessing to me.

When we arrived, the nurse tried to set my IV, and it didn't go well. My veins are small, and they roll, so it took four sticks before they finally got it in. By this time, I was distraught in my heart. I wanted to be well and not have to walk down this dreadful path. It was a six-hour treatment but we were there literally all day.

As I entered the treatment room, it was filled with recliners and there was an atmosphere of heaviness. There were seven people already in the room with their treatments underway. I went to a corner recliner near the back of the room and the nurse began my treatment. She said she would keep a close watch on me since many people have adverse reactions to the chemicals. She asked me to let her know if I had shortness of breath, itching, hives, etc. I tolerated it and tried to calm down once it was underway.

I began to look around the room and I wondered about each person's story. The other patients were of all ages, and each person had his or her own burdens to bear. We were all in one room fighting for our lives and I felt we all shared an unspoken bond.

As I sat in my recliner with Herbert by my side, I began to thank God for my blessings. First, that God would never leave me nor forsake me and then for the gift of my devoted husband. I can't tell you the importance of what his love and commitment meant to me. He told me over and over that we would get through this together.

I also knew my daughters were at home praying for us. It was a very challenging time for them because my prognosis was not good. They are both saved and living for the Lord, so they too were trusting God to see us all through this trial.

It was especially hard for our daughter Kelly because she her son was almost two years old and she had just given birth to a set of twin boys. They had to be cared for in NICU for their first week and Kelly had so much on her plate. She needed me more than she had ever needed me in her life. Can you even imagine how strong she had to be? She had just gone through a high-risk pregnancy due to her Type 1 diabetes. Now she was coping with three babies under two years old and a mother who was fighting for her life. Kelly's diabetes was extremely hard to manage during this time because stress seriously affects blood sugar levels. I had to give all of this to God. I couldn't be there for her, but I could ask God to be with her to provide the help she needed. And He was! Her faith was amazing and she was a real trooper. She was in survival mode but was still always concerned about me.

Then my thoughts went to Abby, our youngest daughter. She loves me more than you are supposed to love anyone. I am her hero. What would happen to her if I die? I love her so much and I could not entertain this thought another second. It was time to pray **big**!

I began to pray with a troubled but thankful heart. I was able to communicate with the Lord intimately. I began thanking Him for providing refuge and strength during this raging storm. I felt my heart begin to soar in an upward spiral. God began to lift me out of my sadness and into the heights of His perfect peace and joy. He reassured me and said, "I've got this, Rita. I am your Father. I am in control, and you can trust Me."

I began to think about all of the ways Jesus was transferring my burdens to His strong shoulders. Once again, I was that broken lamb being carried by my Shepherd. My thoughts began to unscramble and I started to rest in His love.

The days following my first chemo treatment raised several questions and decisions about the new path I was taking. I went back to work on the Monday and my manager pleaded with me to continue to work while I took the treatments. He said I could have days off when I had chemo treatments or if I needed to rest. He knew that taking good care of my clients was very important to me. I didn't have a backup, so I agreed to work through it all. Hindsight is 20/20 and if I had it to do over, I would probably take the time to slow down and take better care of myself, but I didn't. I pushed through and asked God to carry me. He gave me peace as I woke up each morning to face another day. My friend, Jo Rayshell, was a source of encouragement as she told me that my cancer wasn't going to ever catch up with me because I moved so fast. I just felt I had to keep moving forward.

I began to notice lots of my hair on my pillow and in the shower. It began to fall out in extreme amounts the first week. My sister Linda came over and suggested that she cut it very short for me. I agreed and it seemed to make it a little easier for me. She took me wig shopping and picked out a darling wig for me. I thought it actually may have looked better than my real hair!

The Lord cares about every detail of our lives. He compelled me to look to Him, and I realized nothing escapes His notice as I read in the Bible in Luke 12:7 that even the hairs of my head were numbered and that I should not fear. I looked sort of incomplete with my bald head, but miraculously I felt complete in my heart. I didn't focus on what I saw in the mirror but on God's unseen hand that was holding mine.

Herbert held onto our marriage vows "in sickness and in health" as we went through the valley of the shadow of death. He encouraged me daily and supported me fully. It was hard to arrive for my chemo treatments and find that because my white blood cell count was too low, I couldn't have the treatment. I would get a shot to help my white count and go home praying that it would work. Other times, my red blood cell count would not be where it needed to be and they would give me another type of shot and send me home. **God helped me walk "on top of the valley" as only He can!**

As I went on with my life at home, church and work, I prayed daily for strength to continue. God spoke to my heart telling me that He was pleased with me. I was being obedient and receiving His blessing of peace that passes beyond understanding in my heart, and I felt His unconditional love shining upon me. I was full of thankfulness and trust as He carried me each day.

Chapter 10

Prayer of Faith for Healing

James 5:14, 15—Is any sick among you? let him call for the elders of the church; and let them pray over him, anointing him with oil in the name of the Lord: And the prayer of faith shall save the sick, and the Lord shall raise him up.

God doesn't leave us to suffer alone. He picks us up and uses other Christians to help carry our burdens through prayer and encouraging words. My sister,

Linda, had a bonfire to celebrate her twin grandsons' birthday. She invited us and we accepted even though I was very sick. I vividly remember standing by the warm fire on that chilly afternoon in December when Linda's son-in-law, Terry Walker, asked me a thought-provoking question: "Aunt Rita, have you considered God's promise in James, chapter five?"

I honestly didn't know what he meant by the question, so I answered, "No, what do you mean?" He went on to explain that the Scripture in James 5:14, 15 says, "Is any sick among you? Let him call for the elders of the church; and let them pray over him, anointing him with oil in the name of the Lord: And the **prayer of faith** shall save the sick, and the Lord shall raise him up; and if he has committed sins, they shall be forgiven him."

Terry had a very serious look on his face. I knew instantly God was using him to speak words given to him by the Holy Spirit. It was a powerful moment where I felt hope spring up inside me. God uses us to encourage and guide one another. When Herbert and I got home, I immediately studied and prayed over the fifth chapter of James. I pondered the words in my heart and asked the Lord to help me process what that meant for me.

The following Sunday at church, I went to Pastor Norris' wife, Mila, and explained the situation. I asked her if our pastor had ever anointed anyone with oil in obedience to James 5:14. Mila smiled sweetly as she compassionately took my hand and said, "Yes, he has when someone has come to him **in faith** asking for this type of prayer." We discussed it further with Pastor Norris and agreed on a time to meet.

I invited our dear friend, Pastor Steve Goforth, to join the men of our church for this special time of prayer asking God to heal me completely and spare my life. Steve; his wife, Sherri, and their precious children, Shane, Stephanie and Katie, are lifelong Christian friends who have always been there for us.

As I prepared for the meeting the following Thursday morning, God was doing a lot of work in my heart. I had learned to trust that I could ask Him anything (small or large), and I knew He would answer me. Each day He renewed my strength and provided me with a song in my heart. I refused to lie in bed and give in to cancer as long as I could put my feet on the floor each morning. So, when Thursday morning finally arrived, I looked in the mirror at my bald head and noticed my complexion was a pale tone of gray, and my eyes were very weak. My mouth had some blisters, and my toenails had turned dark. My eyebrows and eyelashes were completely gone. I think I may have felt a little better than I looked. I got dressed, popped on my trusty wig and out the door Herbert and I went.

We didn't talk much on our way to our church. When we arrived at the church, Pastor Norris, Pastor

Goforth and several other church leaders (John Herdman, David Justice, Jesse Zuniga, Kurt Copeland, and Ken Anderson) were there. They all gathered around me and laid their hands on my shoulders.

Pastor Norris began by saying that he would obey the Scripture of James 5:14, 15 and anoint my forehead with oil. He went on to say that there is no power in the oil, but the **power to heal would come through the faith and obedience** that had brought us there that day. He emphasized verse 15, where the Bible says, "And the prayer of faith shall save the sick." He pointed out that if healing were contained in the oil-anointing act itself, he would walk the hallways of hospitals to heal people. However, that is not the source of the healing: it comes from faith— **faith in God that He is able**. My faith brought me there and because of my faith in God's ability to heal, each man began to pray aloud to ask God for complete healing in my sick and weakened body.

Herbert knelt beside the chair in which I was sitting with tears in his eyes. As each man prayed, Herbert firmly held my hand with his big, strong hand and occasionally squeezed it to emphasize his support for the words that were being lifted up to our Heavenly Father on my behalf. Tears flowed down my cheeks as I felt the presence of the Holy Spirit with us in a mighty way. I knew that Jesus, my Saviour, was hearing our cry for healing.

Jesus has infinite compassion for us. When He walked on earth, He was moved with compassion for the sickness and burdens of the people He met. He could just speak and people were healed immediately. I believe every miracle in the Bible and we were asking God for another.

Then something wonderful happened. Our assistant pastor, John Herdman, was praying aloud for me and I suddenly felt a coolness rush through my body. It started at my feet and flowed to my head. It was not cold chills—it was a coolness that is inexplicable. I didn't say a word, and tears continued to pour down my cheeks. I felt total peace. Somehow it was different than I had ever felt before.

Jesus was speaking to me with a particular authority that I had come to recognize as the Lord's own voice through the Holy Spirit saying that I was healed. Somehow I knew that, like it had happened for the woman described in Luke 8:43–48, Jesus' power had provided me with immediate healing. As He told her that her faith had made her whole, He was whispering the same words to me through the Holy Spirit that lives in my heart. As Jesus told her to go in peace, He also told me.

Wow! I was speechless. Each man continued to pray until all seven men had asked God for my healing. When they finished, Herbert got up from kneeling beside me. Through his tears, he humbly thanked each of them. I couldn't say a word.

On our drive home, we were both very quiet. Herbert's heart was broken by my illness, and it was such an emotional time.

Thoughts of what had just happened were rushing through my mind. **I felt like I had been sitting on the steps of death's door and that my Shepherd had come and rescued me once more.** How could I describe what had just happened?

I began to tell Herbert about what I had experienced. I told him I believed that the Lord had touched me and healed me. He responded with a glance at me and I saw the look of hope in his eyes. We just rode the rest of the way home very quietly.

When I got home, I didn't really want to talk about what had just happened. I just wanted to bask in the feeling of total peace that was still engulfing me. I was forty-nine years old and had never before felt like this.

I knew in my heart that God had done a mighty work and from that moment on, cancer was just the circumstance that had brought me from my darkest hours back to a place of peace and joy.

Chapter 11

Declaring the Works of the Lord

Psalm 118:17—I shall not die, but live, and declare the works of the LORD.

I continued to pray and ask God to help me understand this miracle. I am an ordinary woman, but I know the supernatural power of God. His Holy Spirit works in me and through me. I had become the recipient of a miracle that was beyond human comprehension.

I pondered it over and over in my mind. I thought it might be best to keep it to myself because people might dismiss it, thinking I was in a rose-colored world. Many people would say I was doing so well because of my positive attitude. I have been known for seeing the silver lining in the clouds that came my way, but my healing was not a result of positive thinking. How could I ever explain that I was healed because God had actually performed a miracle?

As Herbert and I rode to Nashville a few days later for the next chemo treatment, I remember Jesus giving me courage and peace as He comforted me with His unseen hand. In my mind I sang over and over the song "Blessed Jesus, Hold My Hand." I felt at peace, yet I also felt like there was something else I needed to do. I couldn't get clear direction, but I knew He had something else He wanted for me.

Once we arrived and they were administering the treatment, I felt a sudden prompting from the Holy Spirit. I urgently asked Herbert to hand me my Bible. He gave it to me. I held it and prayed, asking God to give me clear direction for my life.

I didn't go to the concordance or flip through the pages. I opened it up, and my eyes went directly to Psalm 118:17, which says, "I shall not die, but live, and declare the works of the Lord." God had given me a message with emphasis and clarity. I knew it was the voice of the Lord. He had a plan for me. I got so excited and told my precious husband that God's purpose in my cancer was not for me to die—but to live and tell everyone else what He had done for me.

I began to think back to the year before when He completely healed me of a very aggressive breast cancer. I had been obedient by becoming a "more fruitful fig tree," but I had never talked much about my miraculous healing. Now God had taken a step even further and miraculously healed me of advanced metastatic ovarian cancer. **My mission became clear that I was to** *TELL* *about the power God demonstrated when we ask Him to move mountains in our lives.*

What a glorious day it is when we walk in obedience to God's Word and live out the Scripture that the apostle Paul wrote in Philippians 4:6. He told us to take everything to God in prayer and supplication with thanksgiving. Prayer is asking and thanking God. I think it is so important to remember to thank Him for everything.

When I left hospital that day, my direction in life had changed forever. I would "declare the works of the Lord" from that day forward. My mission on earth was clear: to tell others about God's great power that can come to us by simply asking; all the while, believing that He can, and desires to, deliver that power to us.

I want to give God the glory and honor for answering our prayers. My motivation for sharing my story comes from a deep, heartfelt desire to give God the honor for sparing and blessing my life. Also, I want to encourage others to learn dependence on Him through a stronger prayer life. **He wants us to ask Him for everything the way a little child depends on his earthly father for every need.**

As we grow in the Lord, we begin to recognize and respect His power and revere His majesty. When I realized my weakness and unworthiness, He manifested Himself to me, providing His strength in my heart and in my life, thereby allowing me to honor Him. He can do the same thing for you today. God hears and answers our prayers when we diligently seek Him.

With my new found mission on earth to "declare the works of the Lord," I asked God to help me accomplish that mission. What does living after a miracle look like? God answered me quickly by giving me Luke 17:11–19. This account of Christ's healing ten men told me that I must live out my life with a thankful heart. Like those men, I had come to Jesus asking in faith for healing and mercy. With simple obedience, I received blessed results.

Luke tells us that Jesus entered a village where He encountered ten men who had leprosy. They asked Him to have mercy on them, and He healed all ten of them. The Scripture says that only one fell on his face at Jesus' feet to thank Him. The other nine didn't come back to give Him thanks. God spoke loudly within my heart at that moment and told me always to be that *one*. I should spend the rest of my life giving thanks at the feet of Jesus. If I am positioned at His feet and never elevate myself, I will feel His presence over me. I can thank Him for every breath I take and thank Him for every situation in life. Thankfulness and humility became the fundamental attitudes guiding my life.

As Paul wrote in I Thessalonians 1:4, "Knowing, brethren beloved, your election of God," I knew with all confidence that we had asked God to heal and He had answered our prayers and had also given me a mission. I began to tell almost everyone I met about the power of asking God and how He had worked miracles in my life. Our relationship with God is such a personal one. I prayed and asked God to give me boldness about sharing my new testimony of His power.

Revelation 12:11 says we overcome Satan by the word of our testimony. Hence, I am writing in addition to telling it because "the dullest pencil is better than the sharpest mind."

I think it is so important to know that God wants us daily to ask for everything, not just for the miracles that we need in our lives. I developed a deep desire to declare the works of the Lord in my everyday life, not just in the dark and desperate days.

Chapter 12

The Good Shepherd

John 10:14—I am the good shepherd, and know my sheep, and am known of mine.

I am so thankful that I had a Shepherd to **carry** me when I needed it and now that I could walk again, I had a Shepherd to **follow**. I continued to be obedient when God led me to give my testimony of His healing in my life. I was so excited and thankful to be alive.

It had been about five years since my first cancer diagnosis. My mother knew her prayers had been answered because she reached ninety years of age in 2009 and I was still alive. We celebrated her ninetieth birthday with a party, and she loved it. Throughout the year, I could see her health beginning to deteriorate.

Since I was a little girl, I had dreaded the day Mama would die. She was such a huge part of my heart, and she made me feel like everything was right with the world when I was in her presence. I remember one night when I was young she came to my bedside when she heard me crying and asked why I was upset. I told her through my tears that I was afraid she was going to die because her hair was so grey and she seemed so old. She reassured me that she would not die until she was very old and I should go to sleep.

She was right. She was ninety and I knew her time was drawing near the end. What could have been the most sorrowful time in my life actually turned out to be a sweet time with the Lord. It was the day the Good Shepherd took my mama to Heaven. Death had lost its sting as Jesus paved the road to a beautiful home-going for her. We knew that she was not going to cross Jordan alone.

One week before she died, her doctor told her that her heart valve was completely worn out and she had only a short time to live. He asked her if she would be willing to sign a "Do Not Resuscitate" form. We were in her small hospital room on a Friday morning. I will never forget it. She looked to me with her questioning eyes and then at Misty, my niece, as if to say, "Are you ready for this?"

We knew for sure that when her heart beat its last beat, she would not want to be in the hospital with the chaos of doctors shocking her heart while her family stood in the hallway. We discussed it, and she bravely chose to sign it. We all agreed that she should be at home with her children, grandchildren and great-grandchildren.

They processed her paperwork, and we went home in an ambulance together. I held her precious, little hand as we took the ride to her house. She knew the end was near because, even though her heart valve was worn, she still had a keen intellect. I could feel her processing what the doctor had said. She seemed at peace with the thoughts of going home to Heaven, and I didn't sense any fear at all. What a strong Christian woman! I could never have asked for a better mother to be an example for me.

Her heart valve lasted one week after that trip home in an ambulance. The following Friday afternoon, we were all there with her when she was ready to take her last breath. We all gathered round her bed and held hands. We softly sang her all-time favorite song, "Angels, Rock Me to Sleep."

Angels, rock me to sleep in the cradle of love.
Bear me over the deep to Heaven above.
When the shadows shall fall and the
Saviour shall call,
Angels, rock me to sleep
in the cradle of love.

When we finished the song, my sister Linda led us in a prayer in which she told the Lord we were at peace if He was ready to take Mama home to Heaven. When the prayer was over, she had peacefully slipped away. She was not afraid or anxious. My beautiful, treasured mother was finally with Jesus.

Even the day of her funeral and burial was so comforting. It was a very still, bluebird sort of day. As the men began to lower her casket into her grave, a strong, gusty wind came blowing through the cemetery. We all looked at one another as if to say, "What was that?" But then we all felt comfort and thought maybe the Holy Spirit of God, our Comforter, was emphasizing the fact that He was with us. It reminded me of the sound of the rushing, mighty wind in Acts 2 when the disciples were all filled with the Holy Spirit. It was such a strong wind that it blew over most of the floral sprays on stands that stood around the grave. We were so moved by the gift of His presence that we began singing. As they lowered Mama into the grave, we broke out in praise and sang "Amazing Grace," followed by "I'll Meet You in the Morning."

The day that I had always thought would be the worst day of my life was full of peace and comfort. I will always miss Mama, but I embraced her death because it was such a powerful testimony of a praying mother. God gave me a gift of comfort that day that I will always treasure.

I began to live claiming Philippians 1:20, 21:

"...that with all boldness, as always, so now also Christ shall be magnified in my body, whether it be by life, or by death. For to me to live is Christ, and to die is gain."

I realized that, because of God's power, we are winners either by life or by death. My message had to be: there will always be sickness among us, but it does not have to have dominion over us. We must ask God to heal and restore our health and then *trust His answer*. He can teach us so much through sickness and pain if we trust completely that He is in control. Sometimes our most blessed testimonies come from our suffering.

Ultimate healing will come to all Christians when this life is over and we are all made whole as we enter Heaven's gates. My friend, Michele, claims this promise of God as her comfort since her husband, Doug, went home to be with the Lord at the age of forty-six. She continues to be a faithful example of what God calls us to be in our time of sorrow. She is a godly mother of three, a schoolteacher and a precious friend to many. The light of the Lord continues to shine through her, even in her darkest hours.

I had asked Jesus, the Good Shepherd, to carry me through life's storms, and He did. I knew that I had been left here on earth for a purpose.

Through my experience with near-death, I had learned that it was entirely up to me to place myself in a position to be able to hear from God. He is always present. I was listening in a new way. I wanted to grow in a new capacity to serve Him.

I began to confess more than ever my inadequacies to the Lord and ask Him to help me. My need and desire for recognition continued to diminish, and my self-worth began to come more from God than from my accomplishments in my position at work. I realized that heretofore much of my self-esteem had come from my accomplishments in the corporate world. I began to realize the things that really matter are deeply rooted and dependent upon my personal relationship with God the Father, the Son, and the Holy Spirit. He is my Father who hears and answers prayers. He is an omniscient, living God who hears the cries of Christians and knows our hearts. He sees our faith. He knows our sincerity.

I have learned that He provides divine intervention in natural affairs. His work is miraculous, supernatural and has no limits. He has patiently taught me to ask Him for all that I need because He is a God of infinite love and mercy.

He is the Good Shepherd, and He knows His sheep. He hears and answers the prayers of those who diligently seek Him. I don't deserve to have my prayers answered, but I am a forgiven sinner. We are all sinners, but God loves sinners. His love and grace are boundless.

When you accept Christ and believe that God hears and answers prayers, you hold the secret to the very heart of God. You, by faith, can find all of the graces, powers and majesty of the one true and living God.

I began to try to make more time in my day to spend alone with God. While taking long walks or sitting very still I could hear Him best. He is eager to hear your prayer today. It is in the very nature of God to answer our prayers, no matter how unworthy we may feel.

At this point in time, I hadn't really thought about how my life could influence other people. I had made so many mistakes that required God's forgiveness, and it was my weakness that revealed God's strength to me. Once He forgives our sin, He puts it as far as the east is from the west. I realized that, (even though my life had so many ups and downs,) what I had gone through could be used by God.

I know His voice, and I know that His goal for me is wholeness, complete confidence and peace. I asked God for clarity to know where to go next in my life. The Good Shepherd led the way.

Chapter 13

Facing Our Giants

*II Chronicles 20:15b—Thus saith
the LORD unto you, Be not
afraid nor dismayed by reason
of this great multitude; for the
battle is not yours, but God's.*

When we are born, we are innocent and without
judgment. We don't know if we are a boy or girl. We
don't even know we have arms and legs. Our lack of
knowledge doesn't matter to us. We are precious
babies who don't know that we are all totally
different from one another.

As we grow, the world tends to categorize us.
People begin to group us by our capabilities, our
appearances, our place of birth and rearing, and other

criteria. If we allow them, people may influence how we regard ourselves. However, if we will rise above the pull of the world and turn to God, He will guide us to see ourselves the way He sees us. He loves us the way we are, but He loves us too much to leave us that way. He will provide us with healthy self-esteem—better yet, with a biblical view of who we are in Him—if we put our trust in Him, not in what others think of us. God wants us to accept His unique creation of each of us. His incomprehensible love is coupled with that acceptance. He also gives us an internal ever-present need for spiritual growth.

Regardless of circumstances, if we are to find true joy and happiness, we must manage our emotions and responses according to His will. Accomplishing this does not come by accident or by luck, but by spending time with God daily. There are no short-cuts. Prayer and meditation on God's Word bring us into the presence of God. Thus we have His help in overcoming our struggles.

Right from the beginning, my life began with struggles that required God's help. When I was born I had polio. It was a mild case and was not discovered until I was nine months old.

It was during a visit from Daddy's brother, Tillman, his wife, Mary, and their new baby girl, Rose Marie, when it all began. Daddy loved it when they came to visit from Maryland. It was their first visit since my birth, and Aunt Mary was excited to see her new niece for the first time.

As my mother tells it, Aunt Mary was shocked to see my terribly crooked legs, as I stood holding the railing of my crib. She asked, "What in the world is wrong with this baby's legs?" My mother didn't know what to say. She knew there was a problem, but she had not sought out a doctor. She was hoping my legs would gradually straighten on their own. She had prayed diligently for me to be healthy and normal, like her other five children. I think I always held a special place in Mama's heart because I was her baby—her baby that needed lots of prayer.

It was obvious to Aunt Mary that something was terribly wrong. I think God sent her to us as an answer to Mama's prayers. Aunt Mary immediately made an appointment at Vanderbilt Hospital. Together, she and Mama took me to see a doctor. He put me in braces that I wore until I was almost four years old.

I vividly remember being a little girl with crooked legs. I really didn't mind, because I was so happy I could walk. I remember people talking about my legs. It didn't bother me. I felt fortunate not to be in a wheelchair, like the children I would see on the March of Dimes commercials on television. I also felt blessed, because it seemed to me that my condition prompted Mama to give me an extra measure of love.

We all have things about us we cannot change. Most of us have something we would like to change about ourselves, and being content with who we are is not always easy. Once we accept who we are, we realize our differences make us special and unique.

As a young child, I realized I could always look around and see someone less fortunate. I have often thought about the positive impact that early experience made on my life. Thankfully, the braces were successful. I have a special place in my heart for Mama's faithful prayer life and for Aunt Mary who cared so deeply for me. She was a busy lady and had Rose, her own beautiful baby girl, yet she made sure I got the care I needed. I am glad my mother asked God for help—and that He sent it.

Life is a series of ups and downs. God can use us to help others when they are down or in difficult situations, if we are in tune with His voice. It is amazing how much we can influence other people's lives if we just take the time to listen and obey.

God puts people in our path, and it is up to us to open our eyes to recognize this. All of us will experience points in our lives where we will need the support of others. These hard times often lead us to have a compassionate heart. The Lord wants us to recognize the needs of others and be sensitive to them.

Sickness and hardships come as giants that give us the opportunity to help others. I tried to encourage others as I lived with my doctors saying my cancer would most likely show up again. I lived as bravely as I could as I continued to face this giant. As the years passed, my oncologist continued to insist I have CT scans of my chest, abdomen, and pelvis every ninety days. He said that cancer can hide and then rear its ugly head somewhere else in the body.

These scans began in 2004. It felt like I spent most of my time in the doctor's office getting scans and blood work. The seven years following my diagnosis, I had four scans a year. Each one reminded me of God's healing.

My doctor was concerned about me, but he was also concerned about my daughters. On several of our visits, he would bring up the subject of genetic testing. Though I was the only one with ovarian cancer, there were many cases of breast cancer in my family. If I carried the BRCA gene, then Kelly and Abby could possibly carry it too.

I agreed to the testing for the BRCA gene, which predisposes women to breast and ovarian cancer. The results proved positive. The BRCA gene had been passed down from my father's side of the family. I thought about all of the women in my family who had breast cancer. My father's mother and only sister, my sisters, (Janice and Charlotte), some of my cousins had experienced it, and now I had too. I began to thank God that there was a chance the outcomes in my daughters' lives could be different. I knew my cancer was not random. It was genetic. Having this knowledge gave us power to make decisions. Proverbs 3:6 tells us to acknowledge the Lord in all our ways and that He will direct our paths. With the BRCA gene confirmed, I needed the Lord to direct my path. I knew I was at very high risk of having cancer in my other breast. My doctor strongly suggested that I should be proactive and move forward with a bi-lateral mastectomy... (easy for him to say). I labored over it because it seemed so drastic. I asked myself over and over, if you don't have cancer now, why go to such extreme measures? Then I recalled how I felt when I was diagnosed the first time. Did I really want to go there again?

Have you ever heard anyone say, "Everything is going great in my life, so I think it is time to make a change?" No, you probably haven't and neither have I. It is usually when we are in a valley that we reflect on our lives to make changes. It seems that when we walk the difficult paths, we search our hearts, and draw closer to God. I asked God to lead me and help me make this decision.

That is when He gave me II Chronicles 20:1-30. According to Chronicles, Jehoshaphat was in a tough situation with no great options. He prayed and asked God for deliverance. God came through for him.

When Jehoshaphat entered the valley, the enemy had completely destroyed themselves. God certainly works in mysterious ways! It took Jehoshaphat and his men three days to collect the valuables left behind. He called it "The Valley of Blessing." I knew that God could turn my battle into a blessing.

When I was up against a struggle that could shatter my dreams and cause me to fear, I couldn't let my faith disappear. This was a giant lurking over me. I began to ask God to deliver me. Peace replaced my fear. I knew what I needed to do. **He reassured me that this battle was not mine, but His.**

With God's leadership and peace in my heart, I made the difficult decision to have a bilateral mastectomy and reconstruction. Herbert agreed, and we moved forward with surgery in 2009. Recovery from the surgery was painful, and I had a complication which resulted in an additional surgery. It was a long healing process. I was relieved when it was all over. I knew that I had overcome the cancer giant that had always been standing before me.

I went to Knoxville to visit Kelly. She had made the decision to be tested for the BRCA gene. More than anything in the world, I hoped my daughter's test results would be negative. I knew I had done what I thought I should, but I couldn't stand the idea of her having to go through this too. Unfortunately, her results were positive. She prayed with her husband and they discussed her options. They decided that, in light of all of the terrible ways cancer had affected our family, she would be proactive.

She had three active boys. The timing would never be perfect for her to have such major surgeries, so they decided not to delay. She immediately scheduled a complete hysterectomy and a bilateral mastectomy, followed by reconstruction. She was brave and never looked back. She said she felt it was what she had to do, since she had an 87 percent chance of having breast cancer and a 45 percent chance of ovarian cancer after testing positive for the BRCA gene. Watching my daughter suffer was difficult, but God blessed her with great surgeons and medical staff. It all went well, and now she lives in peace that breast and ovarian cancer will not have the opportunity to wreak havoc in her life.

Abby, my younger daughter, and Nathan prayed about what to do. They made the decision that she too should be tested and she too was positive. It seemed radical in many ways to think that at such a young age, she would walk down the path of a hysterectomy, a bilateral mastectomy, and reconstruction. Her doctors were totally encouraging and supported her. She was a real trooper. Her recovery went well and she got it all behind her.

Once the surgeries were over and all three of us were healed, we moved forward in our lives without the looming clouds of these towering giant of cancer hovering over us. Kelly, Abby and I all felt a sense of relief the surgeries were behind us. God provided us all with peace and confidence that these were the right decisions for our lives. Now we could enjoy our blessings, fully recovered and ready to face the future. We praised and thanked God for hearing and answering all of our prayers through these uncertain days of our lives.

How did we get to the level of complete trust in Jesus?

I think it began with simple faith. Matthew 17:20 tells us that our faith can be as small as a mustard seed, yet have great power. Jesus told the disciples that someone with even a tiny bit of faith (even the size of this small mustard seed) has enough to live a faith-filled life. A little faith is all you need when it is planted in God. When we are new Christians, our faith may begin small, but it is still faith, and God honors it when it is rooted in Him. If you truly believe He is listening when you pray, you have faith. Faith is not complicated and it grows as you see God work as He answers your prayers.

God led me to greater faith through my surrender of time to be still and know that He is a big God. It is the path that leads to knowing Him: it required me to be reading the Bible every day and going to His throne in prayer. This is where I discover renewed strength and nourishment for my soul. I talk to God in prayer about everything from guiding my actions to providing for my needs.

I also specifically ask Him for help with the following things:

- Strength and power to make changes in my life.

- Guidance on how I can better serve Him and others.

- Direction on how to be humble and serve others.

Those who have fallen away from asking for God's help through prayer often lose their passion to embrace His help. **With simple faith, be still and start again. It can fill you with a renewed strength to face the giants in your life.**

Chapter 14

Finding Contentment

Hebrews 13:5b Be content with such things as ye have: for he hath said, I will never leave thee, nor forsake thee.

So where am I now?

As I sit at the traffic signal tapping my fingers on my steering wheel, my heart pounds as I wait for the light to turn green. Then, suddenly, I realize, I'm not in a hurry. What? I've been in a hurry for thirty years. I take a deep breath and realize I'm only going to the grocery store. It's not urgent. Can this wonderful life be my new reality since my obedience to God in leaving my job? It seems to be a life that has found favor with God. My life no longer feels like I am stewing in a pressure cooker.

God has strengthened and settled me. Now I feel I am enjoying double blessings through which I can live my life and minister to others.

I am walking in God's will for my life to the best of my ability. He has put His desires in my heart. I feel I have lived a life of preparation for this time in my life.

When my perspective of what ranked in importance changed, contentment filled my soul. When I listened closely and gave up what I thought was security, I found God's strong arms there to hold me. I have found contentment in God alone.

It was 2014 when I left my career on the altar of sacrifice to the Lord. So what does my new life look like now? There are times when I miss the people, but since the morning I closed my work laptop for the last time, I have never looked back with regret. I now find more time to be alone and focus on my relationship with Jesus.

Amazingly God instantly began to increase Herbert's business and miraculous things started happening. I continue to stand in awe how the years since my leap of faith in leaving my job have truly been the richest years of my life spiritually, while God has met our physical and financial needs in the most unusual ways.

In Luke 12:22-32 Jesus tells us that our Heavenly Father knows what we have need of and when we seek Him, all of these things will be added unto us. The scripture tells us that life is more than concerns about food, clothing or shelter. It is our faith that gives us confidence to be completely dependent on His provisions. He has been so faithful to provide for us.

In John 14:15 Jesus says if you love me, you will obey my commandments. When we trust and obey, total contentment can be found. It is one of God's greatest blessings!

I also enjoy the blessing of more quality time with my husband, children and grandchildren. This was difficult when I worked full-time, but now I am living fully in the moment with my family. Listening. Hearing. Praying. I am focusing on the life in front of me rather being distracted by thoughts of my job.

Even though Kelly lives three hours away, we are so close: she calls me every morning. It is so nice to have plenty of time to chat with her without multi-tasking while we talk. I love that I can sit totally relaxed while listening to her share the things going on in her life as I gaze out the windows of our home. I am also able to make more trips to visit them. She and Andy stay on the go with the boys and their sporting activities. It is always fun to spend time with them.

Abby lives just a few minutes away, so we visit more often now. Actually, another "obedience blessing" involves Abby. She and I had started a children's etiquette business in 2008 called "Southern Grace." God has opened so many doors for us and we have more opportunities than we ever had before. It has been amazing! It is so much fun to work with my daughter. Abby and Nathan frequently visit us with their children, Dylan and Easton. We have so much fun together. Our oldest grandson, Dylan, spends a lot of time with us on the weekends.

Since I left my job, God has quieted my heart and corralled a lot of my energy. I have been able to focus better, as the Lord has helped me to manage my time and energy. My friends, Amanda Stephan and Becky Browning, encouraged and supported me to complete this book. In their own unique ways, they have been like special gifts sent directly to me from Heaven.

It is important how we start life, but what is even more important is how we finish. We all sin and fall short of the glory of God, but it is important to finish well. I want to be like the apostle Paul in II Timothy 4:7 and finish strong for the Lord. At the end of Paul's life, he said, "I have fought the good fight, I have finished the course, I have kept the faith."

As I have spent more time with God, He has shown me ways to better finish my course. He recently revealed some of my shortcomings I had been too busy to see in the past. I realized I talked too much and listened too little. By listening more closely to God, I have also learned to listen better to others and understand their needs.

It doesn't come natural for me to be a good listener, but I have realized the importance of it. I am embarrassed when I think of the times in the past when I have spoken, but should have been listening. I consider those an opportunity to apply the principles of letting go of the past and press on to do better now and in the future with God's help.

I started listening closer to what my husband was saying and looking for ways to help him. There are very few times that my husband has physically needed my help with anything, especially hay deliveries. I am not exactly a farm-hand kind of girl. I like to work in the flower garden, but that is about as far as it goes. However, on an extremely hot July day, he could not find anyone to help him and he had a good customer in need of hay. He was desperate for help, so I offered to assist.

As we began to unload the fifty-five pound bales of hay in the extreme heat and humidity, my heart began to palpitate and I began to sweat profusely. I hoped it was just the heat. Panic raced through me. I felt like I may be about to have a heart attack. I began to think I could die right then and there.

I was too stubborn to tell Herbert. He needed me to help him, so I just kept stacking bale after bale. With the possibility of disaster staring me in the face, I prayed and I asked God to help me. Rescue me, please, Lord!

We were at a very remote, secluded farm in the country. The barn was down a very long lane in the middle of nowhere. As crazy as it sounds, we looked up and a red pick-up truck was speeding up the drive. A tall, lumberjack sort of looking man jumped out of his truck, leaped up on the hay trailer and started helping Herbert unload the hay. He told me to go sit down and that he would take it from here. Then strangely he said that he was driving down the road and just thought there may be someone who needed help. What? That was so random! How could he have known? I suddenly knew The Lord had heard my prayer and sent help.

I went to the office in the horse barn and the lady there who owned the farm said she had never seen him in her life. She was as confused about who he was as we were. Herbert didn't know him and had never seen him before either.

I sat down in the air-conditioned office and rested until I felt better. When I came out they were finishing up. The smiling stranger asked if he could pray with us. With his big, strong hands, he reached out for our hands. There the three of us held hands and he began to pray to God thanking him for me and Herbert. He asked God to bless us and thanked Him for us living Christian lives.

The strangest part of the story is that we don't know this man and have no idea how he could have known what kind of lives we were living. He prayed for us for several minutes. I was praising God in my heart that He sent this man. It was just crazy! I told him how grateful I was as he had come there. We never heard from him again and have no idea who he was. I just know for sure that I asked God for help and he heard and answered my prayer.

Trusting God fully has brought some exciting things to my life. It has also brought joyful things like singing. I joined the choir at my church. It has been such a blessing to me, as we bless others. I really can't sing very well or read music, but I love to praise and worship God as I make a "joyful noise." Psalm 100 says to make a joyful noise unto the Lord and to serve the Lord with gladness and to come before his presence with singing. Music helps to express my praise and thankfulness to God for all He has done for me.

When God healed me from the storms of cancer, He used music to encourage me. I played one song on a CD over and over. It was "I'm Not Afraid of the Storm" I played and sang it over and over. I truly was given courage when I trusted Him. The song reminded me of the scripture in II Timothy where Paul tells us God hasn't given us the spirit of fear, but of power, love and a sound mind. I no longer feared cancer.

God allowed me to walk through this painful experience because He wanted me to remain faithful through it. I let go of things I couldn't control and trusted Him. This can be an encouragement to others and draw them nearer to Him.

So many blessings continue to pour into our lives. Having more time has afforded me the opportunity to exercise God's gift of hospitality. Using our home to host and serve missionaries warms my heart. It is my opportunity to be a blessing to people serving God on the frontline.

Also, when I was working, I couldn't fit in time to be a volunteer to help others on a regular basis. Now, I look forward to most Fridays when I can serve meals to the homeless at the Journey Home with my faithful friend, Kathy Hoover. This is such a blessing for me. It helps me to be the hands and feet of God. Having a servant's heart is what He wants for us. Our relationship with Jesus is strengthened when we follow His example of serving others.

Now I am free to enjoy the life God planned for me. In 2016, God called me to begin a ministry for ladies called Marriage Matters. I felt the strong urging of the Holy Spirit to obey the command in Titus 2:3, 2:4.

The aged women likewise, that they be in behavior as becometh holiness, not false accusers, not given to much wine, teachers of good things; That they may teach the young women to be sober, to love their husbands, to love their children.

I prayed and asked God to provide what we needed to help our obedience to this calling come to fruition. He answered in a mighty way and provided so many friends to be supportive of it in every aspect. Misty Keninitz writes the curriculum and teaches, while Gail Wrather helps provide refreshments, and Susanne Adams is our prayer leader. Robin Wrather is the coordinator. We also have a faithful Christian lady share her testimony each month as an inspiration for each of us. It has been amazing!

God has also provided faithful friends, (Linda Stoner, Betty Lane, Debbie Rowland, Nancy Burton, Susanne Adams, Betty Rowland,) to be table leaders for the girls. We use my home to invite ladies to come monthly for a two-hour meeting to encourage them to stay strong in their marriages. Our goal is to strengthen marriages and break the cycle of brokenness in homes. We want to encourage women in knowing that their marriages matter according to God's plan for marriage as provided in Scripture (Genesis 2:18-24).

I think it is important to teach women what the Bible says about marriage and make the connection to what that looks like as we apply it to our daily lives. (Titus 2:3-4) In our group we learn from one another through accountability, prayer and support (Proverbs 27:17; I Thessalonians 5:11).

This ministry has become precious to me as I see all of us looking for ways to be godly wives.

Herbert and I continue to enjoy attending church under the leadership of a faithful pastor. I believe that attending a doctrinally sound church on a regular basis helps to keep me encouraged and grounded. In Hebrews 10:25 we are told not to forsake the assembling of ourselves together but to exhort one another. In Ephesians 5:25 the Bible states that Christ loved the church and gave himself for it.

I have found that even more of my spiritual growth comes from spending time very early in the mornings with the Lord. I feel like it is a divine appointment where I meet with God and He prepares me for the day ahead. This time alone with the Lord is my favorite time of the day. He fills my cup with truth, peace and joy. I love to spend this quiet time reading the Bible and communing with Him. I have stopped doing things FOR God and started doing things WITH Him. He leads. I follow.

I continue to examine myself daily and ask God to reveal any sin hiding deep in my heart. God faithfully brings things to my mind. Each time, I realize my ugly sin, I confess it and ask The Lord to forgive me. Joy fills my heart as I feel His love and forgiveness rush over me. I think I had just been too busy in the past to clean all the dark corners of my heart.

After experiencing these last three years of spiritual growth, I began to feel a new sense of confidence. It was a renewed confidence in myself through Jesus. Then God gave me a very special blessing in October of 2017. While Herbert and I were visiting Israel, we made our way to the Jordan River. I felt a strong urging of the Holy Spirit to be baptized. Yes, I was baptized in the very river where John baptized Jesus. It was the most intimate, spiritual moment of my entire life. It felt so right to rededicate myself to God and follow with baptism with a clean, renewed heart.

Isn't it just like God to provide the perfect Bible Study for such a time as this in my life? During this season of my life, our Bible study group is right in the middle of *All Things New: A Study of II Corinthians* (written by Kelly Minter). It has been such an inspirational study of how Paul tells the church at Corinth that because of Jesus the old has gone, and the new has come. It confirmed that now my life should be used by God to give what I have, give who I am, and to live my life to encourage others to follow Christ.

What a great feeling to desire a pure heart and walk in obedience. Isaiah 64:6 says that our righteousness is as filthy rags. When we accept Jesus, He imputes His righteousness to us as a gift. I do not deserve anything, but as a Christian I get what Jesus earned and deserved. So, when I pray, I go to the Father and ask it all in Jesus' name because I am not presenting who I am, rather I pray through and by the authority of Jesus Christ, my Saviour.

Herbert and I stroll, hand-in-hand, into our future with confidence, as we continue to ask God to lead the way and provide for us. We ask Him to give us hearts to respond when He opens a door of opportunity to witness as He leads us.

We share a genuine thirst for God's plan for our lives. We feel the overwhelming presence of the Lord as we seek to serve Him daily.

We know God saw my sacrifice and Herbert's faith, and the Holy Spirit spoke to my heart to let me know the Lord is well pleased.

When each of us, with simple faith, learn to ask God about the direction He wants our lives to take, the course of our lives can be forever changed.

The Eye of the Storm

When life's raging storms are all around,
When no peace at all can be found,
Be still and know that God is near
To calm the worry, pain and fear.
In every storm there is an eye
Where Jesus is quietly standing by.
He whispers, "Dear child, please come inside.
While the storm is raging, in Me abide.
I'll take your troubles and work them out.
Just trust in Me and never doubt.
You have My Father and you have Me—
A safer place you can never be.
Just look to Us and you'll be safe,
Riding the storm and using your faith.
Looking to Us on bended knee,
Yes, you will experience VICTORY!"

Janice Freeman

I Am Loved

Without hope I am afraid.
I often wonder who's to blame.
My heart longs after Him who calls,
who rescues me before I fall.
My heart grows weary.
I cannot speak.
My sin is great.
I feel so weak.
I try so hard.
I fall so deep.
All I want to do is weep.
I give my pride;
He takes my hand.
We walk along the promised land.
I will not run; I will not hide,
because I know who walks beside.
I stood ashamed with broken walls
built up so high I could not see
the pain that was inside of me.
I looked above to see Him there—
Standing, waiting patiently.
Broken, shameful and afraid—
He took the blame.
He spoke my name.
I was so close to the grave;
but with outstretched arms, He **forgave**.
He picked me up and brought me home
and said, "You'll **never** be alone."
I cried so hard, my eyes grew red.
I could not hear what He had said.
He spoke again with gentleness,
"You'll never be alone in this."
My spirit flew above the clouds
where Mercy knew no shame, no doubt.
My head no longer droops below,
for God has washed me white as snow.
I feel so **free**.
How can it be?
His love is ever pouring.
I will not run; I will not hide,
because my God resides inside.
He gave me hope from above,
so I'll never doubt that
I am loved!!

Liz Campbell

Made in the USA
Lexington, KY
05 June 2018